The MONOCLE
Travel Guide Series 18

Berlin

For more information, please visit *gestalten.com*
———
Bibliographic information published by the Deutsche Nationalbibliothek: The Deutsche Nationalbibliothek lists this publication in the Deutsche National-bibliografie; detailed bibliographic data are available online at *dnb.d-nb.de*

Monocle editor in chief and chairman: *Tyler Brûlé*
Monocle editor: *Andrew Tuck*
Books editor: *Joe Pickard*
Guide editor: *Mikaela Aitken*
———
Designed by *Monocle*
Proofreading by *Monocle*
Typeset in *Plantin & Helvetica*
———
Printed by *Offsetdruckerei Grammlich, Pliezhausen*

Made in Germany

Published by *Gestalten*, Berlin 2017
ISBN 978-3-89955-679-7

© Die Gestalten Verlag GmbH & Co. KG, Berlin 2017

Welcome
—— Berlin in
your pocket

Berlin: the home of currywurst, techno and debauchery, right? It may be the city's reputation but visitors will soon discover that there's much more on offer than *sausages* and excessive *revelry*.

For a long time Berlin lacked the wealth and stability of other capital cities so ingenuity prevailed. A broad-minded approach to cultural infrastructure and funding saw an influx of *creatives* – and with them the emergence of vibrant and edgy art, design and music scenes. It's now known as a place where creativity is fostered, resourcefulness encouraged and *originality* embraced.

The low barriers to entry also benefitted independent retailers, the technology start-up scene and, more recently, restaurateurs. Over the past few years talented chefs have been quietly converting the city into a *culinary haven* with a culturally diverse spate of restaurants.

And then there's the knack that Berliners have for repurposing wastelands, abandoned airports and dilapidated buildings. An opportunity is seldom missed to create engaging communal green spaces, rule-breaking hotels or pools with underwater sound systems. *Wunderbar!*

Through persistence, Berlin has forged a new *identity* and grown its own wealth; few cities can rival its verve and tenacity. It's a place that begs to be explored so turn the page and let us introduce you to its most winsome charms. — (M)

Contents
—— Navigating the city

Use the key below to help navigate the guide section by section.

H Hotels

F Food and drink

R Retail

T Things we'd buy

E Essays

C Culture

D Design and architecture

S Sport and fitness

W Walks

Map
—— A tale of one city

The landlocked German capital is divided into 12 sprawling boroughs, each with their own version of a city centre. Don't let this vastness deter you though: navigating Berlin can be a breeze. Here are a few fast facts that will help forge your bearings before you touch down.

The city has been standing since the Margraves of Brandenburg founded Berlin and Cölln as neighbouring trade cities in the 13th century. Over the course of history the two merged (Cölln became Neukölln in the southeast).

A more recent influence on the geography was the East-West divide. Old embassies, regal residences and upscale shopping precincts lie in the western neighbourhoods of Charlottenburg and Tiergarten. The edgy counterculture and notorious nightlife hangouts are found in Kreuzberg and Friedrichshain in the east. In the middle is Mitte, the ideal starting point for iconic sights, cultural must-sees and retail outposts.

WEISSENSEE

Flea market
and karaoke
in Mauerpark   KulturBrauerei

PRENZLAUER BERG

Volkspark
Prenzlauer
Berg

LICHTENBERG

MITTE

• Alexanderplatz

Volkspark
Friedrichshain

TV Tower

Museum •
Island

Spree

Frankfurter Tor

FRIEDRICHSHAIN

Checkpoint Charlie

East Side Gallery •   • Haubentaucher

Jewish Museum
Berlin

KREUZBERG   RUMMELSBURG

Oberbaumbrücke
WRANGELKIEZ   • Badeschiff

Landwehrkanal

ALT-TREPTOW

BERGMANNKIEZ

Soviet War
Memorial

PLÄNTERWALD

NEUKÖLLN

Tempelhofer Feld

BERLIN SCHÖNEFELD
AIRPORT

BAUMSCHULENWEG

TEMPELHOF

Hufeisensiedlung

0   1km   N

Need to know
—— Get to grips with the basics

There's a lot to take on board if you're planning a trip to the German capital. Is there any kind of cultural hangover from the days when Berlin was a city divided? Where can you grab a snack on Sunday when most of the shops are closed? And is it true what they say about Germans and their perceived lack of a sense of humour? Read on for our map of possible pitfalls and top tips on how to avoid them.

A city divided?
Geographical states of mind

Postwar, occupied Berlin was famously divided into east and west. These days the physical split has disappeared, save for a ribbon of bricks where the Berlin Wall once ran, but an imaginary wall still exists in the minds of many. Even younger people born in the West aren't usually enticed by the East's post-wall hipness, and easterners find the west a bit staid.

Still, there's another divide fewer visitors and newbies notice: north versus south. Kreuzbergers or ultrahip Neuköllners in the south wouldn't be caught dead in bobo Mitte or Prenzlauer Berg in the north. Berliners tend to stick to their neighbourhood so the city can feel like several villages stuck together.

Casual everyday
What to wear

The notion of Berlin sartorial style includes lots of black, asymmetrically cut clothing, utilitarian boots and undercut hair. Much of the cliché rings true but for the past decade or so, smart suits and tailoring have made headway in certain neighbourhoods such as Mitte, the Tiergarten government district and Charlottenburg.

Anything goes in the daytime but in general, don't go too formal in the evening. In the majority of Berlin bars, clubs and other night-time venues, those dressed in corporate or conservative wear get the side-eye or might not get in at all (some exceptions do exist, by the way; simply check the cool factor before venturing out).

Buy now
Shopping hours

Berlin retail has changed dramatically in recent years. While closing time was once 18.00, now it's 20.00 (in some cases even 22.00). Unlike the rest of Germany, shops in Berlin can open on selected Sundays too (on a non-shopping Sunday, go to the supermarket at Hauptbahnhof or Friedrichstrasse train stations). Also unique to Berlin are corner shops with extended hours selling drinks and snacks. These *spätis* (*spät* means "late") can be lifesavers.

I always do my annual kerchief shop in Berlin

Get out of the way!
Care on the roads

Traffic in Berlin is, in a word, unfriendly, but things are much easier if you follow certain rules. *Do not* stand or walk in the bike lanes on pavements (generally marked with darker bricks or a painted line): you'll incur the wrath and loud bells of bikers and possibly be run over. If on a bike, do not leave your path and venture into traffic – German drivers tend to accelerate, not slow down, for stray cyclists or jaywalking pedestrians.

I feel I add a certain regal flair

Curb your sarcasm
Say what you mean

When talking to Germans in general and Berliners in particular, irony of the British sort doesn't wash. It's met with confusion at best or shock at worst. The nonliteral is a nonentity; understatement goes undetected. A recent *Economist* article on the topic said many expats speak to Germans "in as straightforward a manner as possible, as if they're talking to Siri on an iPhone". So don't say you could eat a horse unless you are actually planning to.

Shake it all about
Handshakes and introductions

Berliners are not famous for their genteel manners but a few tips will make socialising here easier. In business meetings or more formal settings, offer your hand and your name, even if you've met the person before. Handshaking is big throughout the German-speaking world. Not all Germans introduce each other so it's best to take the initiative and do it yourself. But at private parties, doing such a thing too soon is considered forward and slightly awkward, especially in the cooler, younger scenes. Wait until you've struck up a conversation and then introduce yourself ("By the way, I'm Tom"). Also refrain from asking about your conversational partner's profession until a bit later, if at all. Such a thing is considered to be very Anglo-Saxon and a little pushy.

Water, water everywhere
Outdoor swimming

Berlin might be landlocked but the German capital has more than 100 options for outdoor swimming on hot days. Within city limits are 80 lakes, including Wannsee, Europe's largest inland beach. Its east Berlin counterpart is the vast Müggelsee. Smaller lakes include Plötzensee in Wedding and Krumme Lanke in Steglitz.

Then there are outdoor pools such as the trendy Badeschiff, set directly into the River Spree in Friedrichshain, and the incredibly hip new Haubentaucher pool, which doubles as a music venue. Topping things off are a few public baths, while architecture firm Realities United is working with the city to put a pool into the Spree near Museum Island.

That's enough of your lip
Berliner Schnauze

"Berliner Schnauze" is a term for the "snouty" way a lot of natives talk: a gruff, barky, lippy vernacular that sounds coarse coming from bus drivers and shopkeepers. But really chat to those speaking this way and you'll usually find a cheeky Berliner just going with the flow.

Service round up
Tipping

Servers in Berlin are usually paid fairly and service is embedded in restaurant prices. Simply round up your bill (a couple of euros if the bill is moderate; for larger bills, around 5 to 10 per cent for good service is the norm). Do this while paying; it's not usual to leave money on the table (important: *zusammen* means paying together, *getrennt* means each guest pays his or her own way). Tip around 10 per cent to taxi drivers, a euro or two to bell staff in hotels.

Be a friendly guest
Good neighbours

Berlin recently banned most Airbnb rentals. In part, this policy move is a reaction to hordes of short-term visitors marauding on stag or hen nights through neighbourhoods such as Neukölln or Kreuzberg and throwing parties in otherwise residential buildings. Locals have in some cases pushed back with anti-tourist behaviour. A tip: be as considerate a guest in Berlin as you can be. Remember, people live here. They'll (usually) return the respect.

The neighbours are going to love this..! And Iiiieeeeiiiii will always love yoooouuuuu...

Hotels
—— Where to hang your hat

The grand buildings of Berlin suffered greatly in the 20th century, turning into shells of their former selves. Hoteliers, however, found opportunity among the rubble and began repurposing the once faded and forgotten buildings into a mixed bag of stately and innovative offerings.

Even among the more orthodox ilk there are fascinating backstories: luxurious Das Stue is a former embassy, Hotel Oderberger was a public bathhouse and Hotel de Rome a 19th-century bank. And then there are the rule-breaking ventures that have refreshed the hotel template and opened in old apartments and factories: Gorki Apartments, 25hours and Michelberger.

Today the German capital has no shortage of smart and welcoming hotels to rest your head; the only difficulty is trying to decide which beguiling neighbourhood you'd like to stay in.

1
Michelberger Hotel, Friedrichshain
Rock'n'roll digs

When this hotel opened its doors onto Berlin's late-night neighbourhood in 2009, a steady stream of music-industry heavyweights rolled in. Nights were debaucherous and guests rarely roused before noon. "The band thing was a pleasant accident," says creative director Azar Kazimir. "We've grown up a little now and so too has the hotel."

You'll still spot bleary-eyed musos who have been holed up in the band room (yes, there is a purpose-built band suite) but families and business travellers also populate the homely hotel. Its biggest attribute is the absence of stuffiness. Staff are friendly and accommodating, the café, courtyard and restaurant are relaxed and rooms, although petite, are playful and cleverly configured. Leave space in your luggage for a bottle of Michelberger schnapps and an in-house-designed T-shirt.
39-40 Warschauer Strasse, 10243
+49 (0)30 2977 8590
michelbergerhotel.com

MONOCLE COMMENT: If travelling with a large contingent, opt for rooms 204 and 304. Designed by Sigurd Larsen, they each have a maze of bedrooms, bathrooms, a sauna, kitchen and dining area.

Hip but happy
——
The hotel prides itself on friendly service

I'm ready to jam.
Which way to the band room?

Hotel Amano, Mitte
Neighbourhood trendsetter

Hotel Amano was the first offering by Ariel Schiff and Artur Süsskind when they launched their Amano Group back in 2009. Found close to the centre of Mitte, its location alone is a major draw – you can fall out of bed in the morning and land in a trendy gallery, café, restaurant or bar without much effort.

The accommodation covers 163 functional, minimalist rooms and serviced apartments; the interior design has been ably handled by Berlin's Ester Bruzkus Architects (check out the displays by photographer Oliver Rath).

The rooftop bar, open during the summer, attracts Berlin's beautiful people but you'd be wise to take advantage of its sister venues too. Just around the corner you'll find Hotel Mani, which has a restaurant of some renown, while Hotel Zoe has a bar dedicated to gin in all its many varieties.
43 Auguststrasse, 10119
+49 (0)30 809 4150
amanogroup.de

MONOCLE COMMENT:
The Amano's rooftop and its adjoining conference room have been known to moonlight as a yoga studio, fashion week runway, cinema and live music venue.

②
Das Stue, Tiergarten
Flawless design

This stately hotel is a classic building in the diplomatic district of Tiergarten. The former Royal Danish Embassy was built in the 1930s by Stuttgart-born architect Johann Emil Schaudt. Meaning "living room" in Danish, Das Stue was converted into a 78-room hotel by Axthelm Architects and decorated by Spanish designer Patricia Urquiola.

Besides the main lounge that hosts jazz on Fridays, there are three libraries, a 14-metre swimming pool, a sauna, a spa and a 24-hour gym. The hotel also boasts a private entrance into the neighbouring Berlin Zoo, whose resident elephants can be heard and occasionally glimpsed from the windows.
1 Drakestrasse, 10787
+49 (0)30 311 7220
das-stue.com

MONOCLE COMMENT: Although the concrete floors and white tablecloths in house restaurant Cinco feel slightly sterile, the food is anything but: Catalan chef Paco Peréz plates up Michelin-starred Mediterranean fare. You can watch the master and his team at work through large windows that look into the kitchen.

④

Hotel Adlon Kempinski, Mitte
Royal occasion

Opened by Germany's last
emperor, Kaiser Wilhelm II, in
1907, this luxurious hotel became
a refuge for heads of state and
prominent figures; guests have
included the British royal family,
Albert Einstein and Marlene
Dietrich. After burning down
during the war it was rebuilt 90
years later in the same priceless
location by the Brandenburg Gate.

Today the five-star venue
belongs to the Kempinski hotel
group but it still has the air of a
family-run establishment: doormen
and receptionists know the names
of returning guests and loyal
patrons. With 307 rooms and 78
suites, as well as three restaurants
including the two-Michelin star
Lorenz Adlon Esszimmer (Le
Petit Felix is a more casual affair),
nothing here is lacking, especially
when it comes to the Royal Suite.
It will relieve you of €25,000 per
night but with its 24-hour butler
service, bulletproof windows and
view of the Brandenburg Gate, it's
certainly not your average room.
77 Unter den Linden, 10117
+49 (0)30 22610
kempinski.com

MONOCLE COMMENT: If you're
after some pampering, head to
the Adlon spa: an entire wing is
dedicated to treatments such as
massages, facials and manicures.
You can even book your own Spa
Suite and spend the day hopping
between a Finnish sauna and a
Jacuzzi.

5

Soho House Berlin, Mitte
Exclusive elegance

This 1920s Bauhaus building
was designed by architects Georg
Bauer and Siegfried Friedlander.
Originally a department store, it
was retooled as a headquarters for
Nazi brownshirts in the Second
World War. Postwar, it became
home to the Communist party
Central Committee before being
left unoccupied after the unification
of the city in 1989. It wasn't until
2010 that the storied heritage
building was finally converted
into Soho House Berlin.

Today the establishment
offers 65 rooms and 20 serviced
apartments and also rents out
four loft apartments on short or
long-term leases. As to the facilities,
guests and members of Soho
House can enjoy a gym, rooftop
pool and the Club Bar (which
has an art deco vibe), while two
restaurants serve US and Aegean
dishes respectively. Another
restaurant serves Italian fare and
is open to the public. The spa is
run by UK skincare company
Cowshed and all rooms are
stocked with its products.
1 Torstrasse, 10119
+49 (0)30 405 0440
sohouseberlin.com

Global club
——
The first Soho
House was
founded in
London

MONACLE COMMENT: The four 250
sq m lofts are among the biggest
suites in town. Guests can choose
between a two-bedroom or three-
bedroom abode fitted with a full
kitchen and sit-in bar, floor-to-
ceiling windows and of course, DJ
decks. This is Berlin, after all.

⑥
Hotel de Rome, Mitte
Style in the bank

If you're looking for a rooftop with a view, the best one in town is Hotel de Rome's, situated in the heart of the city overlooking the State Opera House. Another institution with a storied history, this listed building once served as the headquarters of the Dresdner Bank.

It has a swimming pool housed in the former jewel vault where, at the turn of the 19th century, ladies would pick up their Sunday pearls; its black wall tiles resemble the safe boxes that once stood here. The grand ballroom is located in the old stately cashier's hall and the oak-panelled suites lie in the offices and conference rooms of the former bank directors, complete with leather-padded doors, hidden bookcase-passages and in-room safes (you can also get your nails done inside the bank's main vault, which makes up part of the wellness area today).

The Rocco Forte Hotel group has taken pains to ensure that the hotel's history is preserved across its 145 rooms – even its shrapnel-scarred walls remain intact, in memory of the Second World War.
37 Behrenstrasse, 10117
+49 (0)30 460 6090
roccofortehotels.com

MONOCLE COMMENT: Reserve a table at the hotel's Italian restaurant La Banca, run by executive chef Jörg Behrend, for an authentic Mediterranean experience.
The icing on the cake: seasonal ingredients and olive oil sourced from its own farm in Italy.

High appeal
—
The building has five storeys and excellent views

⑦
Miniloft, Mitte
Home comforts

Miniloft is situated in Berlin's happening Mitte, only a short stroll from the Berlin War Memorial, the Natural History Museum and the feted Schlot jazz club. It offers little apartments that resemble a home away from home rather than a hotel room. Each miniature loft – of which there are four categories, including Extroverted, Introverted, Classic and Compact – is furnished with a fully equipped kitchenette and dining area.

The interiors of the concrete-floored rooms are just as minimal and functional as the exterior (which won the owners, architects Matthew Griffin and Britta Jürgens, numerous awards for its stainless-steel extension). "We created what we couldn't find anywhere else at the time," says Jürgens.
5 Hessische Strasse, 10115
+49 (0)30 847 1090
miniloft.com

MONOCLE COMMENT: The classic studio apartments, located in the renovated part of the building dating from the 19th century, are quieter than the contemporary additions and exude more charm thanks to the old brick walls paired with modern furnishings.

⑧
25hours Hotel Bikini Berlin,
Charlottenburg
Cosy and cosmopolitan

You know a hotel is doing
something right when the city's
residents frequent it as much as
the guests. This branch of the
formidable 25hours Hotel group
attracts Berliners in droves thanks
to the pastries hot from the oven
at the on-site Woodfire Bakery
and the numerous freelancer
workspaces and meeting rooms.
Then there are the panoramic
views from the 10th floor, where
restaurant Neni Berlin serves a
Moroccan, Middle Eastern and
Russian fusion menu and the
Monkey Bar stirs a stiff sundowner
and hosts nightly DJ sets.
    In addition to spacious rooms
flooded with natural light from
floor-to-ceiling windows, guests
receive free bike and BMW Mini
rental, speedy in-room wi-fi
connectivity, guided Thursday
morning runs and a sauna.
40 Budapester Strasse, 10787
+49 (0)30 120 2210
25hours-hotels.com

MONOCLE COMMENT: Choose
between the cityscape vistas in the
Urban Rooms or Berlin Zoo views
in the Jungle Rooms. We prefer the
Jungle options, which come with
windowside hammocks.

Appetising greens
Choice
dishes and
top views
at Neni

Art hotel
—
In 2016 Schlosshotel turned part of its building into a gallery with a rotating programme of photographic-art exhibitions. The hotel works in co-operation with photo publisher TeNeues and notable Berlin-based galleries to compile shows inspired by fashion, nudity and architecture.

⑨
Hotel Q!, Charlottenburg
Scandinavian style

Named for its proximity to Berlin's premier shopping mile – the Kurfürstendamm, also known as Q-Damm – this gem designed by Berlin-based Graft architects was one of the city's first design hotels when it opened in 2004. Characterised by organic shapes and wave forms, monochrome colour palettes and minimalist furniture, this 77-room establishment run by Michael Schön and Kian Shams-Dolatabadii is a good pick for those seeking to explore the lively side of the city.

The communal areas are always buzzing: the leafy interior courtyard is packed on barbecue evenings in the summer months and, as Shams-Dolatabadii says, "For many guests our lobby is almost their living room." The Fox Bar is also a popular stop-in for locals and visitors alike (we strongly recommend the bubbly house cocktail).

Each room features amenities by Rituals. When you've had enough for the day, put your feet up by the lobby's fireplace or head to the wellness area, which even includes a relaxing "mini-beach".
67 Knesebeckstrasse, 10623
+49 (0)30 810 0660
hotel-q.com

MONOCLE COMMENT: If mornings are not your thing, check into one of the Standard with Bathtub rooms: you can practically roll right out of bed and into a bath.

⑩
Patrick Hellmann Schlosshotel, Grunewald
Creative refinement

The Schlosshotel sits in the quiet – and somewhat exclusive – Grunewald neighbourhood. Built in 1914, it has a disjointed design history: back in the 1990s, the building was given a makeover by fashion icon Karl Lagerfeld and most recently several rooms have been refreshed by fashion and interior designer Patrick Hellmann.

For the most part the public spaces are paeans to early-20th-century elegance – they've been much favoured for fashion shoots. The 43 rooms and 10 suites, meanwhile, tend to be a little more subdued; Hellmann's renovated rooms have a New York theme with a minimalist monochrome palette accented by splashes of colour.

Facilities focus on luxurious relaxation, with everything from a spa with forest views to a cigar lounge; one suite even has its own library. Active guests can take advantage of nearby tennis courts, while the staff can recommend nearby horse-riding and organise bespoke cycling tours or a simple map of the nearby forest for joggers.
10 Brahmsstrasse, 14193
+49 (0)30 895 8430
schlosshotelberlin.com

MONOCLE COMMENT: As well as a limousine service for airport transfers and shopping trips, Schlosshotel offers the use of a Rolls-Royce Ghost with its own chauffeur.

11

Gorki Apartments, Mitte
Self-contained luxury

These two five-storey buildings were erected in the early 1900s and once home to some of Berlin's Golden Age theatre darlings. However, like much of Mitte they withered while the city was divided, but were revived half a century later when Gorki took up residence and opened in 2013.

The pied-à-terre-style accommodation offers 36 apartments, two of which are capacious penthouses sleeping six to eight guests. French-German architect Sandra Pauquet spearheaded the design, taking two years to collect the winsome jumble of furniture and trimmings, including pieces by homegrown talent Egon Eiermann. Seemingly small touches like access to a direct doorbell and mailbox help accommodate for long-term stays.

25 Weinbergsweg, 10119
+49 (0)30 4849 6480
gorkiapartments.com

MONOCLE COMMENT: Don't fret over the lack of a hotel lobby. All concierge services, including airport transfers, same-day laundry and bicycle hire, are offered. Comforts such as Paper & Tea brews, freshly baked Friedl biscuits and Dr Bronner's toiletries are further perks.

Nice neighbours
───

Weinbergsweg has seen a spate of restaurants and independent retailers opening in the last few years. Enjoy breakfast at Gorki Park, pick out your favourite magazines from Soda (*see page 59*), eat an ice cream at Süsse Sünde and pick up some new threads from Rotation.

⑫
Hotel Oderberger, Prenzlauer Berg
Trendsetting heritage

"Hotels are all the same ultimately – I often don't know which country I am in," says Barbara Jaeschke. "Here every room is singular." She opened Hotel Oderberger in 2016, in the leafy Prenzlauer Berg neighbourhood just around the corner from the Kulturbrauerei.

What is now a cosmopolitan hotel was originally established in 1902 as a public bathhouse. The grand building, designed by architect Ludwig Hoffmann, was fitted with a pool and enough baths to serve the neighbourhood. "When we emptied the place we were left with a pile of 300 bathtubs," says Jaeschke.

It took €20m to transform the building into a luxurious hotel while sympathetically preserving its unique architectural identity. Sandstone archways, ornamental stair rails and the iconic white tiles and mint-green changing room doors have been incorporated into the design of each room – and the magnificently restored pool is the centrepiece.
57 Oderberger Strasse, 10435
+49 (0)30 780 089 760
hotel-oderberger.berlin

MONOCLE COMMENT: Keep an eye out for the photographs by Johanna Keimeyer that decorate the hotel's walls: fittingly each picture from Keimeyer's "Pool Around Me" series is an underwater scene taken in more than 75 hotel pools around the world.

Alternative stays

01 **COJE, Neukölln:** The process for building the combined accommodation and workspace called COJE was fraught with creative disagreements, jokes Marcus Kolata, who worked on the project with his wife and fellow designer Isabella. "We fought for five months," says Marcus. Happily, it was worth the angst. The duo converted an open-plan industrial-style space into an indoor village of 10 wooden cabins with a communal kitchen and living area. It is designed to host meetings, film shoots, family gatherings and corporate retreats however, single occupancy is also possible.
coje-berlin.com

02 **Tautes Heim, Neukölln:** Graphic designer Ben Buschfeld and his wife Katrin Lesser had long admired urbanist Bruno Taut's Horseshoe Estate *(see page 116)* when they found a house in the compound that was for sale. "It was in a poor state and in urgent need of restoration but it was a real treasure," says Buschfeld. Following strict conservation practices, it was opened to the public as a guesthouse for up to four people, decorated with furniture from the 1920s. "It's a stimulating place that offers an alternative to impersonal hotels."
tautes-heim.de

Hey, dogs can cat nap too...

Food and drink
—— Top tables and bar stools

As Berlin's once wildly independent arts and music scenes have settled down, creatives have been turning their attention to food and quietly converting the city into a culinary hotspot. Traditions born from Prussian heritage, west Berlin's French fixation and east Berlin's Vietnamese diaspora were first thrown out, then rediscovered and expanded on as the post-reunification influx of people from across the globe brought with it original ideas about food.

New openings still abound, though increasingly the most exciting ones take place in Neukölln or Wedding rather than well-established Mitte and Kreuzberg. The result is a food scene that's culturally diverse, strong on concepts and concerned about sustainability and organic agriculture – all reflected in our selection of the best food and drink the capital has to offer.

❷
Nobelhart & Schmutzig, Kreuzberg
Locavores rule

Berlin chefs have been making a point of celebrating Germany's produce for some years now but nobody has gone as far as Micha Schäfer and Billy Wagner. The young chef and the famously outspoken sommelier gained much attention when they opened Nobelhart & Schmutzig in 2015 and declared they would use exclusively local ingredients – so no pepper, lemons or olive oil allowed. It may sound frugal but the dining is anything but.

The restaurant could pass as a funeral parlour from the street but inside the atmosphere is intimate: diners sit at a counter that wraps around the open kitchen and watch the chefs at work. The set menu features 10 or so tasting dishes starring interesting flavour combinations: think cherries and wood sorrel or potatoes and stout.
218 Friedrichstrasse, 10969
+49 (0)30 2594 0610
nobelhartundschmutzig.com

①
Katz Orange, Mitte
Warm welcome

Ludwig Cramer-Klett, a former investment banker from Munich, says the idea for Katz Orange occurred to him while he was in the Amazon with a shaman. Little surprise, perhaps, that it bears an offbeat, alpine-cabin-meets-Andes vibe.

The former brewery site is fronted by a pretty courtyard with seating; inside, the dining room and cocktail bar boast plenty of cosy nooks. Raising the comfort level further is a meat-centric menu dominated by stews and roasts, although vegetarians will find plenty that pleases too.
22 Bergstrasse, 10115
+49 (0)30 983 208 430
katzorange.com

I'm off to forage: I got a hot tip about some mushrooms

③
Industry Standard, Neukölln
Changing tastes

The idea of sharing plates is still rather foreign to most Germans (as is the concept of evenly splitting the bill). But the multicultural team behind Industry Standard have set out to establish the custom.

Located among hookah bars and betting shops, the venue's haphazard look is more akin to a coffee shop than a fine-dining restaurant – but don't think this means that they aren't serious about food. The nose-to-tail culinary approach draws on French and Mediterranean cuisine: star dishes include steak tartare and gnocchi with lemon and rucola.
83 Sonnenallee, 12045
+49 (0)30 6272 7732
industry-standard.de

④
Tulus Lotrek, Kreuzberg
Hearty appreciation

Max Strohe and Ilona Scholl (*pictured*) share an admiration for French painter Henri de Toulouse-Lautrec, whom they call "a great glutton". But there's more that the founders of Tulus Lotrek have in common with each other: they both like intense aromas, good wine and two courses too many than one too few. Accordingly, they've opened a restaurant in a Wilhelminian-era apartment that could easily pass as their home. Diners can choose from either a short and sweet à la carte menu or a longer set-menu option.
24 Fichtestrasse, 10967
+49 (0)30 4195 6687
tuluslotrek.de

Asian food

A little-known legacy of Berlin's former partition is the distribution of east Asian restaurants: while Chinese emigrants usually settled in West Berlin, the Vietnamese often came on an invitation from the GDR and stayed in the East.

01 Hot Spot, Wilmersdorf: This restaurant stands out for accompanying top Szechuan cooking with excellent German riesling. *restaurant-hotspot.de*

02 District Mot, Mitte: This Vietnamese restaurant serves Saigon street food in a playful, colourful space. *districtmot.com*

03 Qua Phe, Mitte: You'll find this lunchtime Vietnamese hotspot a few streets over from the prime retail offering on Mulackstrasse. The coffee is strong, the *banh bao* (steamed buns) and sticky-rice balls delicious and the service friendly. *+49 (0)30 9700 5479*

04 Preussenpark, Wilmersdorf: On summer Sundays the Chinese and Vietnamese communities set up with portable stoves and plastic plates in this park and serve food to friends, family and – for a few euros – strangers too.

⑤
Rogacki, Charlottenburg
Slippery business

Smoked eel has been a northern German delicacy for centuries but when Rogacki opened its fish smokery in a small Charlottenburg backyard in 1932, it was the district's first. It became one of West Berlin's prime gourmet destinations in the 1970s and 1980s and today the family business continues to sell everything from coffee to cured meats. But the biggest drawcard is still the smoked eel.

Join the mature clientele crowding around standing tables for crab cocktails, mackerel and, of course, smoked eel on toast.
145/46 Wilmersdorfer Strasse, 10585
+49 (0)30 343 8250
rogacki.de

6

Wolff & Eber, Schöneberg
Appetite-stimulating conversation

The publisher and gallerist
Robert Eberhardt (*pictured right,
on right*) had a lot of experience
running cultural organisations but
none in gastronomy when, after
losing his office on Unter den
Linden, he opened Wolff & Eber
in Schöneberg's leafy Bavarian
Quarter in 2015.

After dabbling in Syrian-
German fusion, Eberhardt settled
on homely Brandenburg dishes –
think game pies, roast goose
and potato stew. The menu is
well suited to the wooden interior,
which evokes an old German
tavern but comes with white-
cloth napkins.

Thursday's literary salons
remain a popular occasion
among west Berlin's intellectual
bourgeoisie for highbrow mingling
and late communal dinners.
*15 Kulmbacher Strasse, 10777
+49 (0)30 6881 1018
www.wolffundeber.de*

Beer gardens

Berlin isn't Bavaria – there
isn't much of a traditional
beer-garden culture. That
doesn't mean there aren't
any nice outdoor spaces
that also serve beer.

01 Clärchens Ballhaus,
Mitte: Clärchens Ballhaus
is a sanctuary right in
central Mitte serving
traditional Berlin dishes
and surprisingly good pizza.
ballhaus.de

02 Schleusenkrug and
Café am Neuen See,
Tiergarten Park: These
two beer gardens in
the park both have
water views and serve
grilled meat.
*schleusenkrug.de;
cafeamneuensee.de*

03 Die Fischerhütte am
Schlachtensee: If it's
particularly hot, follow up
a swim in Schlachtensee
lake with a cold brew at
Fischerhütte.
fischerhuette-berlin.de

Naples staples
——
The decor is modern but all else is traditional

⑦
Standard, Prenzlauer Berg
Pizza artistry

Standard's minimalist, dark metal-and-wood interior is so carefully designed that you may wonder how serious they are about their pizza. The answer? Very. The owner's background may be in art but he backs up his claim to provide "authentic" Neapolitan pizza with an oven custom-made in Naples and a Neapolitan *pizzaiolo* (pizza cook) who holds a diploma from the Associazione Verace Pizza Napoletana.

Expect it to be slightly burned around the edges, with soft dough and a thick crust.
7 Templiner Strasse, 10119
+ 49 (0)30 4862 5614
standard-berlin.de

⑧
Lode & Stijn, Kreuzberg
Worth the wait

After teasing Berlin foodies for
months with supper clubs and
pop-up brunch gigs, Dutchmen
Lode van Zuylen and Stijn Remi
finally opened their first restaurant
in spring 2016.

Lode & Stijn avoids the rough
edges and stark decoration of the
city's other newcomers (though the
kitchen is open plan). Instead the
interior is no-frills yet warm thanks
to plenty of blond wood. The same
can be said of the food, which is
only a tad experimental. It's served
à la carte at the bar and as a set
menu in the dining room.
*25 Lausitzer Strasse, 10999
+49 (0)30 6521 4507
lode-stijn.de*

⑨
Big Stuff Smoked BBQ, Kreuzberg
Tastes of Tennessee

Anna Lai and Tobias Bürger worked
as a journalist and a fashion designer
respectively until they visited New
York, discovered American barbecue
culture and decided they couldn't
go back to German-style grilled
meat. So they ordered an oven in
Tennessee and became Berlin's first
seller of hot-smoked meat.

The fillings for their sandwiches
and breakfast tacos (pork belly,
pulled pork, beef brisket and short
rib) come exclusively from German
and Austrian small-scale farmers;
Lai and Bürger keep it affordable
by avoiding prime cuts.
*42/43 Eisenbahnstrasse, 10997
+49 (0)16 3629 0413
bigstuff.de*

⑩
Paris Bar, Charlottenburg
Storied venue

Damien Hirst and Martin
Kippenberger, the legend goes,
have both swapped paintings for
bouillabaisse here. As with most
stories surrounding Paris Bar, it
is near-impossible to confirm. You
won't get an answer from Michel
Würthle, the Viennese artist who
took over the French restaurant in
1979 and still greets his friends and
regulars here every evening.

What isn't in doubt is that the
artists were guests: after all, Paris
Bar has long been the heart of
liberal west Berlin and a favourite
of actors, muses and intellectuals
(Kippenberger depicted the dining
room in his 1991 painting "Paris
Bar"). Following reunification its
patronage declined as diners sought
out new restaurants in the east.

But with the help of new
investors and an improved menu,
guests have been filing back. The
distinguished clientele, always a
little older and more fur-clad than
elsewhere in Berlin, still occupy the
red sofas under the many paintings.
Little has changed except that,
much to Würthle's regret, today
nobody gets upset about the art
on the walls.
*152 Kantstrasse, 10623
+49 (0)30 313 8052
parisbar.net*

 Dóttir, Mitte
Nordic simplicity

This restaurant overseen by Iceland-raised chef Victoria Elíasdóttir is in one of Mitte's last unrenovated buildings. The creaky wooden floors and peeling paint strike a fine balance between artistic improvisation and casual neglect – and create a textured backdrop for the straightforward cuisine.

"I like to use the things that connect me to where I'm from," says Elíasdóttir. "When you work with something that you like – root vegetables, for example – it's about not overcomplicating it. Give the vegetable the chance to be itself."
41 Mittelstrasse, 10117
+49 (0)30 330 060 760
dottirberlin.com

(11)
Lon Men's Noodle House, Charlottenburg
Quick and easy Taiwanese

You wouldn't spend a whole night at this rudimentary Taiwanese spot on Kantstrasse (Berlin's Chinatown) but you can't beat it for quick and hearty meals. Squeeze past the open kitchen with its steaming pots of dumplings to reach the brightly lit, albeit windowless, dining room.

Most people come for the noodle soup, but the chilli wontons and *gua bao* (pork-belly buns) are more noteworthy. It's best to ask for the daily specials, which are not on the menu.
33 Kantstrasse, 10625
+49 (0)30 3151 9678

Fast food

Other than currywurst and döner kebabs, the increasingly popular quick meal of choice for most Berliners is the classic *stulle*. The simple snack of sliced rye bread with butter, cheese and cured meat is experiencing a revival at the hands of artisan bakeries.

Must-try
**Schnitzel from Borchardt,
Mitte:** At Borchardt, plates are large but the schnitzel is even larger. The veal is thin, the breading perfectly crisp and the whole thing is accompanied, as tradition demands, by tepid potato salad. And it bears the stamp of approval from Berlin's members of government, big business, film stars, writers and journalists, who are normally present and seated impossibly close together. They usually come for lunch and so should you.
borchardt-restaurant.de

⑬
Cocolo Ramen X-berg, Kreuzberg
Ramen masters

Following the success of the
Cocolo ramen bar in Mitte –
which boasts consistently long
queues no matter the weather
– Duc Ngo and his team opened
this second outpost in 2013, next
to the Landwehr Canal. It not only
has a larger space but a longer
menu (although bear in mind that
you may still have to wait for a seat
since they don't take reservations).

There are homemade noodles
served in eight different broths,
gyoza, kimchi and a variety of
rice bowls – and soba at lunchtime.
39/40 Paul-Linke-Ufer, 10999
+ 49 (0)30 9833 9073
kuchi.de

Having a bowl
Choose
from eight
varieties of
ramen

⑭
Lokal, Mitte
Neighbourhood favourite

When Maren Thimm and Gary
Hoopengardner closed their lunch
spot Kantine for renovations in
2011 (it's since reopened) there
was a palpable sense of mourning
among Mitte diners – followed by
a sigh of relief when, only a few
months later, they launched Lokal
just a few blocks away.

With its bright dining room,
jumbled furniture and simple
yet modern German food, Lokal
offers a reprieve from the many
conceptually ambitious restaurants
in the area. Ingredients are local
and the menu changes weekly.
160 Linienstrasse, 10115
+ 49 (0)30 2844 9500
lokal-berlin.blogspot.de

⑮
3 Schwestern, Kreuzberg
Simple but effective

Bethanien House was built as a 500-bed hospital, orphanage and nursing school in 1845. It was abandoned in 1970 and later saved from demolition by activists, artists and squatters who repurposed the space as social housing. Today most of the building is used as artist studios and galleries.

This joint occupies the church-like dining hall complete with domed ceilings and arched windows. The food is no-nonsense southern German, with roast pork, schnitzel and *spätzle* (pasta) all mainstays on the menu. During summer, the large garden is ideal for long, lazy lunches.
2 Mariannenplatz, 10997
+49 (0)30 6003 18600
3schwestern-berlin.de

⑯
Bandol Sur Mer, Mitte
Small packages

The dining room here is so tiny that you have to be careful not to knock over neighbouring tables as you take your seat, so you soon develop a sense of familiarity with your 19 fellow diners. This is especially true on weekends when reservations are only possible at 18.00 or 21.00; everybody is served each course at roughly the same time, which encourages conversation.

The modern French set menus (one meat, one fish) are chalked on the walls and it may be the only Michelin-grade meal in town that's set to hip-hop music.
167 Torstrasse, 10115
+49 (0)30 6730 2051
bandolsurmer.de

⑰
Florian, Charlottenburg
Free your tastebuds

This west Berlin institution just off Savignyplatz in Charlottenburg has been in operation since 1982. The name was inspired by Florian Geyer, a freedom-fighter leader during the German Peasants' War in the early 1500s.

The Franconian cuisine features comfort foods such as marinated pork with baked apples, prunes and dumplings, or veal with horseradish sauce, parsley and potatoes. Another drawcard is the unpretentious and homely interior space.
52 Grolmanstrasse, 10623
+49 (0)30 3276 9940
restaurant-florian.de

*Just a small
snack of spätzle
before dinner...*

Must-try
Baumkuchen from Konditorei Buchwald, Moabit:
Baumkuchen (literally "tree cake") is a cylindrical cake made from horizontal layers of thin dough. The recipe dates back to 15th-century Germany.

Konditorei Buchwald confectionery was founded in 1852 and was once supplier to the royal court. Its *baumkuchen* is made with marzipan and apricot marmalade (and exported it to Japan and the US). Enjoy a slice inside the café that feels like a German grandmother's living room.
konditorei-buchwald.de

Pauly Saal, Mitte
1920s glamour

Pauly Saal occupies a former
Jewish girls' school built in
1927 and designed by architect
Alexander Beer. Opened in 2012,
the restaurant is an ode to swanky
1920s Berlin. Murano chandeliers
dangle from the sky-high ceiling,
the parquet floors creak under
waiters' feet and the green velvet
upholstery swallows conversation.
Eyes regularly wander to artist
Cosima von Bonin's huge rocket
suspended on the wall.

Even the classic German and
Austrian dishes are inspired by the
era: the restaurant only serves set
menus and there's a compressed
version at lunchtime. For a more
informal meal head to the cosy
anteroom bar, which often houses
spontaneous afterparties for the
area's many art galleries.
11-13 Auguststrasse, 10117
+49 (0)30 3300 6070
paulysaal.com

Turkish

Döner kebab was invented
in Berlin in 1972 – or so the
Turkish kebab association
claims. True or not, the city's
1,000-plus döner shops make
it a quintessential local food.

01 Doyum Restaurant,
    Kreuzberg: This is straight
    out of Istanbul's old town
    and serves lentil soup,
    meat skewers and plenty
    of strong tea.
    doyum-restaurant.de
02 Balikci Ergun, Moabit:
    An eccentric Izmir-style
    tavern specialising in
    grilled fish that's flown
    in from Turkey.
    382 Lüneburger Strasse
03 Fes, Kreuzberg:
    A modern meat-and-meze
    restaurant with barbecues
    inserted in each table
    and a fine selection of
    Turkish wines.
    58 Hasenheide

*I aim
to have
this
finished
by dinner
time*

⑲
Diener Tattersall, Charlottenburg
Storied halls and stalls

The *bulette* (a type of hamburger)
is to Berlin what Scotch eggs are to
London; consequently Berliners love
to debate which restaurant serves
the best. Many would point to this
riding hall-turned-restaurant, so old
that it prides itself on having served
champagne to emperor William II
after his hunting trips. Since the
1950s it has been owned by former
boxer Franz Diener, who has a knack
for entertainment and liver sausage.

House specialities include Berlin
classics such as pickled herring and
Königsberger Klopse (meat balls
with capers).
47 Grolmanstrasse, 10623
+49 (0)30 881 5329

20

Madame Ngo, Charlottenburg
Hanoi heritage

This "Hanoi brasserie" is the latest
venture from chef Duc Ngo *(see page
34)*, who arrived in Berlin in 1979
at the age of five as a refugee from
Vietnam. Since 1999 he has been
building an empire of restaurants in
the city and in 2016 he decided to
tackle his family heritage. Madame
Ngo, named after his mother, is a
nod to French-Indochina cuisine.

During the day people come
for the banh mi and pho. At night,
elaborate Vietnamese and French
brasserie dishes – think oxtail and
shitake wontons in jus and beef and
hoisin carpaccio – are the drawcards.
*30 Kanstrasse, 10623
+ 49 (0)30 6027 4585
madame-ngo.de*

Food retailers
Bountiful baskets

①
Kochhaus, Prenzlauer Berg
Kitchen experimental

This concept store aims to
encourage people to expand their
cooking repertoires. Inside the shop
there are 18 display tables, each
based around a different recipe;
customers can pick up a method
card and all the ingredients required
to cook each one. The "menu" is
changed weekly.

It's a convenient option for
visitors who'd like to cook one
or two meals during their stay.
Dishes that have been featured in
the past include pecorino ravioli
with chanterelles and Sri Lankan
lamb curry.
*46 Schönhauser Allee, 10437
+49 (0)30 577 089 100
kochhaus.de*

Heavy traffic
Street-food Thursday is always popular

Vintage cheese

Considering west Berlin's close cultural ties with France, it makes sense that Charlottenburg's most famous cheese vendors are Marseille expat Philippe Causse and his daughters. They sell more than 80 types of cheese, tinned sardines and French wine.
maitrephilippe.de

② Markthalle Neun, Kreuzberg
Varied ingredients

This 19th-century market was saved from demolition by local activists and then renovated and reopened in 2011 as a place to sell regional, small-scale and organic produce and for young food entrepreneurs to test their menus. Today Markthalle Neun is the centre of Berlin's food culture.

Farmers' markets take place on Tuesdays, Fridays and Saturdays, though there are also some permanent vendors and restaurants. Additionally there's a street-food market on Thursdays and irregular coffee, cheese and sweets markets.
42/43 Eisenbahnstrasse, 10997
+49 (0)30 6107 3473
markthalleneun.de

③ Erich Hamann Schokolade, Wilmersdorf
Sweet history

This confectionery shop run by a family-owned century-old chocolate manufacturer is a haven for gourmets and aesthetes. Erich Hamann Schokolade still sells its chocolate from the original shop designed by Bauhaus artist Johannes Itten in 1928; the packaging has also kept its fine chequered design.

Be sure to purchase the house speciality – dark chocolate – and try classic German praline recipes such as mocha beans, ginger sticks and cream truffles filled with *kirsch* (fruit brandy).
17 Brandenburgische Strasse, 10707
+49 (0)30 873 2085
hamann-schokolade.de

④ Vom Einfachen das Gute, Mitte
Good provenance

This little shop specialises in simple products of the highest quality. A glass display is filled with cured and boiled hams, sausages ranging from liverwurst to salami and cheese from all over Europe. Fresh bread is stacked behind the counter and at the back, shelves are lined with wine from new and little-known vineyards. The owners pride themselves on knowing each producer and everything they sell comes from sustainable or organic agriculture.
155 Invalidenstrasse, 10115
+49 (0)30 2886 4849
vomeinfachendasgute.com

①
Café Einstein Stammhaus,
Charlottenburg
New ground

During the Weimar Republic,
the Jewish private banker Georg
Blumenfeld hosted aristocrats and
industrialists in this late-19th-
century villa on the quieter end of
Kurfürstenstrasse. It wasn't until
1978 that the building found a
new use: Austrian Uschi Bachauer
opened it as a coffeehouse in the
hopes of reviving the rich coffee-
drinking culture that had existed
in prewar Berlin.

Today elderly regulars, suited
business people and curious
newcomers alike seek out the
wood-panelled rooms to read the
newspaper and eat breakfast that
comes served on tiered stands.
58 Kurfürstenstrasse, 10785
+49 (0)30 263 9190
cafeeinstein.com

②
Engelberg, Prenzlauer Berg
Culinary cruise

At Engelberg simplicity reigns
– and not just in the pleasantly worn
interiors. The standard breakfast
here starts with a basket of bread
plus your choice of Swiss cheese,
Franconian ham and Italian salami,
all cut to order. Bircher muesli,
Bavarian white sausage and *strammer
max* (sourdough bread with
scrambled eggs and bacon, a Berlin
staple) complete the European
breakfast tour.

The café is located on the
sunny side of the street and has a
pretty terrace so it's a nice option
when it's warm outside.
21 Oderberger Strasse, 10435
+49 (0)30 4403 0637
engelberg-berlin.de

Distrikt Coffee, Mitte
Breakfast anytime

The coffee is great but that's not the point. Rather, Distrikt Coffee sets itself apart with elaborate all-day breakfast. The buttermilk pancakes, avocado on toast, poached eggs and inevitable superfood bowls are all so pretty that they could have jumped right out of a lifestyle photo shoot, especially when set against the exposed-brick-wall backdrop.

British-born former science teacher Sophie Hardy and her German partner Hannes Haake opened the space in 2014 in a prewar building. "We source our beans from Berlin but also London, New York, Sweden and Denmark and serve food with a healthy slant, plus home favourites," says Hardy. It's surprisingly quiet on weekday afternoons, when a large table at the back works well for meetings or as a remote office.
68 Bergstrasse, 10115
distriktcoffee.de

conjure the simplistic cosiness of a Tokyo café. They don't serve food but laptops are allowed and the coffee is, of course, spectacular.
70 Adalbertstrasse, 10999
+49 (0)30 2084 88020
bonanzacoffee.de

④
Roamers, Neukölln
Brunch masters

Equipped with just five indoor tables and a very strong sense of aesthetics, Roamers has conquered Neukölln's brunch scene. The intimate space is decked out in rough bleached wood, with plants dangling from the ceiling and cacti, succulents and trinkets occupying every spare inch.

The café serves simple seasonal cakes, eggs, salads and towering sandwiches. All mains are served on wooden boards covered in parchment paper and arranged prettily. Keep in mind that it's cash only.
64 Pannierstrasse, 12043
roamers.cc

③
Bonanza Roastery Café, Kreuzberg
Sipping room

Third-wave coffee shops abound in Berlin but Yumi Choi and Kiduk Reus pride themselves on pioneering the trend. Their roastery and café in Prenzlauer Berg opened in 2007 and was so popular people drank their coffee standing up. Don't fret: this doesn't happen at the newest Kreuzberg location, which is a spacious former carpentry workshop redesigned to

(6)
Salumeria Lamuri, Kreuzberg
Textured experience

The food at this Italian deli, owned
by the former owner of Restaurant
Da Baffi, is uncomplicated. Expect
panini, salad and burrata, plus a
daily lunch menu with dishes such
as vegetable carpaccio or pasta
with pistachio sauce. The location,
however, is exceptional. The former
butcher's shop was renovated to
reveal the original stucco, wall
paintings and floor tiles, giving
the space a charmingly patinated,
Mediterranean air.

Lamuri also functions as a wine
and grocery shop, and the space
can be rented for private group
dinners in the evening.
183 Köpenicker Strasse, 10997
+49 (0)17 5700 3419

*What? It's my
feierabendbier...
taste testing is
thirsty work*

Bread

In 2014, Unesco listed German
bread as a world cultural
heritage, much to the joy of
Germans who've long
considered *brotzeit* (bread with
butter, cold cuts and cheese)
a superior kind of dinner. There
are hundreds of regional
varieties but broadly speaking,
sourdough is more common in
the south, while the north has
wholegrain and dark yeast
bread. Thanks to a revival in
bakeries, Berlin has them all.

In Markthalle Neun (*see page
39*) alone there's Italian Sironi,
famous for semolina sourdough;
Soluna's delicious rye
sourdough; and Endorphina, an
organic bakery that produces a
wide range. Also try the Austrian
cumin bread at Wiener Brot and
the wholegrain at Zeit für Brot.
*markthalleneun.de;
wienerbrot.de; zeitfuerbrot.com*

Drinks
Raise a glass

①

Hops & Barley, Friedrichshain
Beer enthusiasts

This microbrewery has emerged as a favourite among the city's avid beer drinkers since opening in 2008. Hops & Barley combines traditional unfiltered brewing with innovative recipes and natural flavours. On tap are pilsner, dark malts, cider and Berlin-style *weisse* (a wheat beer dubbed the "champagne of the north" by Napoleon's troops).

There's also arguably the friendliest staff in town behind the bar. You'll find a mixed crowd of regulars and football fans (games dominate the screens on match days) in the cosy green-tiled interiors.
22/23 Wühlischstrasse, 10245
+49 (0)30 2936 7534
hopsandbarley-berlin.de

One for the road
Other Germans may scoff at Berlin's beer but they can't fault the beer culture: drinking in public is a deeply rooted tradition. It reaches its apotheosis in the *feierabendbier*, the beer you have at the end of your work day. It's common to enjoy one on your way home on the U-Bahn.

②

CSA Bar, Friedrichshain
Launch pad

This place on Karl-Marx-Allee takes its name from Czech Airlines, the former tenants of the building. Inside you'll soon discover it's not just the name that current owner René Flatau inherited from his predecessors but also a chic 1960s aesthetic. "We've tried to preserve a timeless, classic atmosphere," says Flatau.

With flattering lighting, a laidback soundtrack, comfy leather sofas to fall into and a cocktail list as long as a novel, CSA offers a cosy spot for those looking to hunker down. Stools that span the length of the bar, meanwhile, are an auspicious place to kick off an evening of exploring the surrounding area.
96 Karl-Marx-Allee, 10243
+49 (0)30 2904 4741
csa-bar.de

Out of the woods
──
Locals saved the timber mill from sale

③
Holzmarkt, Friedrichshain
Community project

A neighbourhood co-op purchased this former timber market along the north bank of the River Spree to save it from being sold off to conglomerates. Once completed, the area will feature an artists' village, gardening centre, market, hotel and more. For the time being residents have furnished it with temporary huts of eclectic charm, inside which you'll find a restaurant, espresso bar, co-working lounge and even art exhibition spaces. To best enjoy this favoured summer hangout, pull up a chair by the river and watch the sunset over a drink from Bar Pampa.
25 Holzmarktstrasse, 10243
+49 (0)30 4736 1686
holzmarkt.com

Four more bars

01 Tier, Neukölln: There is no shortage of bars on the street but Tier stands out by virtue of having added a little grace to it. Sure, the yellow table lamps, old wooden tables and soft armchairs are the same flea-market finds of so many Neukölln student flats, but the cocktails are of a rare quality.
42 Weserstrasse, 12045

02 Buck and Breck, Mitte: From the street, Buck and Breck looks like an empty shop; ring the bell that says "bar" and you may be allowed in – provided there's space. When it opened in 2010 it consisted of only 14 stools and no standing room. A back room has been added but it remains one of the more serene places to enjoy a good cocktail.
buckandbreck.com

03 Rum Trader, Wilmersdorf: Waistcoat-wearing Gregor Scholl worships a different era – the 1920s to the 1930s – which is evident in his bar. Fitting only a handful of people, it fills up quickly with men smoking cigars and dapper couples, all of whom Scholl chats with at length. The house speciality is of course rum but other rarities can be ordered.
+49 (0)30 881 1428

04 Schwarze Traube, Kreuzberg: Atalay Aktas once said that it took him and his partners three months' work to get his bar to look so trashy. The quiet man who, thanks to some prestigious awards, is often called "Germany's best bartender" perhaps wanted to make a point: fancy drinks don't require a fancy bar.
+49 (0)30 2313 5569

④
Cordobar, Mitte
Washing away the pain

Cordobar is named after an
incident that in Germany is known
as "the shame of Córdoba": the
dubious 1978 football World Cup
victory of Austria over Germany.
But sommeliers Gerhard Retter
and Willi Schlögl, both Austrian,
offer reconciliation by serving
a remarkable selection of both
Austrian and German wines (there
are normally about 20 open bottles
per night to choose from).
 Come on an empty stomach as
the kitchen serves some of the finest
bar food in town; the black pudding
pizza is a favourite.
32 Grosse Hamburger Strasse, 10115
149 (0)30 2758 1215
cordobar.net

Club scene

No, the Berlin club scene is
not what it used to be – and
yes, you may be turned away
at the door without explanation
– but it's still always worth
trying your luck.

01 Berghain, Friedrichshain:
This famous techno club in
a former power plant is the
Holy Grail for most visitors.
berghain.de
02 KitKatClub, Mitte:
Depending on the night,
the kinky KitKatClub
can offer an even more
interesting experience
than Berghain. Be warned:
to gain entrance you have
to dress the part.
kitkatclub.org
03 Prince Charles,
Kreuzberg: One of the few
clubs to sometimes play
non-electronic music and to
have a swimming-pool bar.
princecharlesberlin.com
04 Club der Visionäre,
Kreuzberg: Located in a
slowly developing pocket
of Kreuzberg, this club has
a charming outdoor deck
over the canal.
clubdervisionaere.com
05 Kater Blau, Mitte:
Kater Blau offers a
taste of fabled Berlin
institutions such as Bar
25 and Kater Holzig.
katerblau.de

*If music be the
food of love...
drink more wine?*

⑤
Rias, Kreuzberg
Refined affair

Rias is one of Kreuzberg's more
grown-up bars with its understated
interior, wood panelling and
barkeepers in black ties. The
atmosphere is both laidback and
welcoming: jazz and swing music
plays in the background and the
drinks encourage you to drop
anchor and stay the entire night.
100 Manteuffelstrasse, 10997
+49 (0)30 5315 7948

Retail
—— Top shops

Berlin has a distinct street style: more casual than Paris, less flashy than New York or London. In the past two decades a spate of young designers have established their labels in the city, all benefiting from Berlin's low barriers to entry and the rise in the global fashion milieu. The result is a seductively independent retail scene.

Beyond the wardrobe there are also innovative concept shops, dynamic specialists and, of course, great record shops. Start your tour of this nascent offering on Mulackstrasse and Torstrasse in Mitte, where standout designers and the shops that support them are concentrated. But don't stop there: use the following pages to map your spree across town from Charlottenburg to Schöneberg, Tiergarten to Kreuzberg.

①
A Kind of Guise, Mitte
German-made brand

"Our aim is to produce high-quality garments and products," says Yasar Ceviker, co-owner and creative director of 2009-founded Munich-based brand A Kind of Guise. The formidable fashion label opened its Berlin flagship in 2015.

Its light-filled space on Mulackstrasse – designed in-house and fitted with furniture by Stattmann Neue Moebel – sells the full range of menswear. Each and every one of its pieces, from knitwear to bags and shoes, is made in Deutschland with fabrics sourced from Japan, Italy and Germany. "The design aesthetic is more or less timeless," says Ceviker. To browse their women's collection, visit Voo Store in Kreuzberg (*see page 51*) or Andreas Murkudis in Tiergarten (*see page 50*).
23 Mulackstrasse, 10119
+49 (0)30 2809 1725
akindofguise.com

②
Herr von Eden, Mitte
Vintage revival

Self-taught tailor Bent Angelo Jensen learnt his trade in the secondhand shops of his native Klensburg, a seaside town near the Danish border. There, the stock of vintage suits provided not only a lesson in pattern-making but also a point of reference for launching Herr Von Eden in Hamburg in the late 1990s.

From dandyism to punk rock, classic tailoring to mod culture, his range of suits, overcoats, shirts and accessories combines a multitude of influences with wearable, contemporary feel and debonair panache.
*33 Marktstrasse, 20357
+49 (0)40 6506 5200
herrvoneden.com*

③
Soto Store, Mitte
Covers all bases

This clean, pared-down shop specialises in menswear. Its first location opened in 2010 along Torstrasse (Soto is short for South of Torstrasse) and expanded two years later into a neighbouring space.

Philip Gaedicke, Omer Ben-Michael and David Fischer, the three friends behind the venture, have a penchant for hard-to-find brands such as Japanese label Bedwin & The Heartbreakers and LA's Band of Outsiders.

Those who are searching for a more staple offering will be provided for by the ETQ trainers, Maison Kitsuné shirts and Thom Browne sunglasses lining the old trunks and industrial shelves (sourced from Amsterdam). We also like the Soto-branded pullover made in collaboration with Converse.
*72 Torstrasse, 10119
+49 (0)30 2576 2070
sotostore.com*

④
AD Deertz, Mitte
Textile discovery

Wibke Deertz's background in fine arts shows through in her sculpted menswear: jackets and trousers are thoughtfully structured, while patterned shirts have a dash of creative eccentricity. "I hope to capture the dynamic spirit of the city in my designs," she says.

Not one for convention, she works in reverse: hunting for leftover textiles and creating small-batch collections from her finds. "I enjoy the sustainability of not ordering or producing fabrics and I absolutely adore the serendipity of finding good stock," she says.

106 Torstrasse, 10119
+49 (0)30 9120 6630
addeertz.com

Womenswear
Feminine fashion

①
Schwarzhogerzeil, Mitte
Trendsetting shop

Your first impression of this Torstrasse shop may be that the fanciable interiors designed by Berlin-based set designer Sylvester Koziolek have been employed to compensate for the minimalist range of womenswear. But fear not: this refined collection, as collated by owner Nicole Hogerzeil, more than holds its own. Expect clothing from German brands Perret Schaad and Felicious as well as the latest collections from Maison Kitsuné and Belgian native Cédric Charlier.

"I started Schwarzhogerzeil at a time when there was next to nothing exciting in terms of fashion retailers in the city," says Hogerzeil. "Demand quickly grew and I'm proud to say that over the years the shop has become a taste-shaping place for many of Berlin's interesting women."

173 Torstrasse, 10115
+49 (0)30 2887 3868
schwarzhogerzeil.de

Does my tartan scarf count as cutting-edge fashion?

② Michael Sontag, Kreuzberg
One-man brand

Designer Michael Sontag founded his eponymous label in 2009, straight out of university. Five years later he decided to become his own exclusive retailer and opened this shop. Since then the brand has become a city favourite. "I've built a loyal client base here," he says.

Sontag describes his womenswear as "ancient goddess meets Berlin" and his sexy dresses and elegant tops drape appropriately over curves. Key pieces reappear each season, with twice-yearly new collections and collaborations such as footwear with German shoemaker Trippen.
41 Muskauer Strasse, 10997
michaelsontag.com

③ Odeeh, Charlottenburg
Fabulous fabrics

Rich fabrics and patterns are the signature of Odeeh. Otto Drögsler and Jörg Ehrlich created the brand in 2008, and opened this shop six years later. The textiles are printed and woven in northern Italy, then sewn mostly in Germany.

"It attracts independent women loyal to the brand," says retail manager Raphaelle Hoffmann. Tailored trenches in woven check and printed silk are wardrobe staples while the luxuriously large soft-wool scarves make excellent travel blankets.
Bikini Berlin, 38-50 Budapester Strasse, 10787
+49 (0)30 2639 1159
odeeh.com

④ Sabrina Dehoff, Mitte
Angles that dangle

After working for designers Alber Elbaz and Cristina Ortiz, Sabrina Dehoff struck out on her own with a fashion consultancy and later a jewellery collection. "It wasn't really planned," says Dehoff, whose first collection of playful golden pendants launched in 2006. "I still see it as a big adventure."

She and three goldsmiths develop prototypes with flashy geometrics and romantic gems as well as manufacturing half the collection. Most of the materials used are sourced domestically.
175 Torstrasse, 10115
+49 (0)30 9362 4680
sabrinadehoff.com

①
Baerck, Mitte
Clothing and more

This concept store can be found on one of Mitte's more vibrant fashion streets, known colloquially as La Mu. Its owners, Ania Bauer and Jacob Brinck, have assembled a modish mix of internationally renowned labels including J'ai mal à la tête and Won Hundred, as well as Berlin-based brands such as Vladimir Karaleev and Goetze. "We try to surprise our customers with the selection," says Brinck.

The space also serves as a showroom for the duo's homeware brand llot llov, which includes lighting fixtures, hanging planters and vases.
12 Mulackstrasse, 10119
+49 (0)30 2404 8994
baerck.net

②
Andreas Murkudis, Tiergarten
Expansive range

Andreas Murkudis (*pictured*) got into fashion retail in 2003 with the opening of his eponymous shop in Mitte. Over time the growing range of products – from clothing and cosmetics to home accessories – outgrew the space available and in 2011 the multibrand shop moved to its current location in Tiergarten.

Hidden in a quiet courtyard, the former printing facility was redesigned as a shop by architect duo Gonzalez Haase AAS. It stocks Céline, Aspesi and Mykita, as well as Susanne Kaufmann's skincare, Werkstatt: Münchenn jewellery and Hohgant's babywear.

"We work with about 200 brands; some sell really well, some sell moderately, some barely sell at all," says Murkudis. "It doesn't matter; we love them."
81E Potsdamer Strasse, 10785
+49 (0)30 680 798 306
andreasmurkudis.com

3

Voo Store, Kreuzberg
Key to perpetual style

A mirrored signboard on the street
directs you to Voo Store located at
the back of a Kreuzberg courtyard,
in a former locksmith's workroom.
Its interior, a hangover from its
industrial past, has been left raw
and expansive, lending itself nicely
to in-house café Companion
Coffee and a calendar of launch
parties and showcases.

But let's not get sidetracked:
Voo Store has one of the city's
most cracking collections of
men's and women's streetwear,
plus a desirable cache of shoes,
accessories, books and homeware.

"We're very fortunate not to be
driven by spreadsheets but rather
by designers and their collections
and what we think our customers
might like," says buyer and creative
director Herbert Hofmann. "We
take a laidback approach and
we don't try to hype trends."
24 Oranienstrasse, 10999
+49 (0)30 695 797 2710
vooberlin.com

Fashion forward

Berlin's designers have a
remarkable camaraderie,
trading tips or simply meeting
as friends. "We help each
other," says Hien Le. "We're
in the same boat with the
same problems – why be
competitive?" Le established
his men's and women's lines
in 2010. His talent for tailoring
has imbued them with a sense
of the essential, placing
quality fabrics and colour at
the forefront.

One of the finest
womenswear labels is Perret
Schaad, founded in 2009.
Designers Johanna Perret and
Tutia Schaad create clothing
that's delicate and feminine in
regards to material and detail,
yet minimal and powerful in
terms of silhouette. "We don't
design for a 'new' woman
but for women to be even
cooler than they are now,"
says Schaad.

Menswear in Berlin is
exciting too. Sissi Goetze's
range, which debuted in
2011, is marked by its lean,
strong lines. Sportswear-
infused elements get a touch
of the avant garde: think
bomber jackets paired with
tapered trousers.

The city's designers all have
a palpable sense of pride and
celebrate their idiosyncrasies.
"Berlin will never be Paris or
London. It doesn't have to be:
Berlin is Berlin," says Le.
perretschaad.com;
goetze.xyz;
hien-le.com

*I share an
appreciation for
fine tailoring*

①

The Store at Soho House, Mitte
While away an afternoon

Berlin is remarkably resistant to organised cool. That said, Soho House seems to have won hearts with help from this shop overseen by London-based creative director Alex Eagle.

A joint venture with The Vinyl Factory, the large ground-floor space has gigantic windows and a jungle of plants. Clothing labels such as Proenza Schouler and Mansur Gavriel, furnishings by Berlin designers and unusual fine jewellery attract customers, while a fine selection of vinyl, a DJ station and overscaled couches invite lounging. In-house restaurant The Store Kitchen is fast becoming a lunchtime favourite too.
1 Torstrasse, 10119
+49 (0)30 405 044 550
thestores.com/berlin

④
Wolfen, Mitte
Democratic fashion

Wolfen has been creating dapper knitwear for men, women and children since 2001. "I started selling the collections to different shops but the clothes became so expensive that I wouldn't be able to buy them myself anymore," says founder Jacqueline Huste. "So I decided to stop selling to others and open my own." She did just that in 2008. The limited-edition clothing, created from natural textiles, is produced in Germany, while knitwear is made in Apolda, a town famed for garment-making during the time of the GDR.
41 Auguststrasse, 10119
+49 (0)30 4978 1966
wolfengermany.com

②
Folkdays, Kreuzberg
Ethical design

After studying development
economics and working in the
not-for-profit sector, Lisa Jaspers
wanted to switch gears. So, while
travelling for work, she began
forming a global community of
artisans and collecting homeware
and accessories. She founded her
socially conscious brand in 2013.

"It was the perfect way of
combining an entrepreneurial
business model with the issue of
poverty reduction," says Jaspers.
"We quickly realised that artisans
were very interested in working
on designs with us so we started
developing product ideas."

Today the range includes
kilim carpets woven in Anatolia,
ikat-dyed silks and jewellery
made from discarded bombshells
from Cambodia.
19 Manteuffelstrasse, 10997
+49 (0)30 9362 6094
folkdays.com

③
Of/Berlin, Bergmannkiez
One-stop design shop

Until recently it wouldn't have
been unusual to return from
a weekend in Berlin with little
more than a hangover and
a colourful Buddy Bear key ring.
Then along came Of/Berlin, a
concept shop selling homeware,
accessories and stationery from the
city's best budding designers.

"There were no shops or
even websites dedicated to cool
souvenirs from Berlin," says Catrin
Soldo, who founded the business
in 2015 with architect Vesna Zaneta
and interior designer Karoline
Ahner (*all pictured, left to right*).
"Nothing represented the
city's creativity."

The trio met at interior-design
firm Minimum but quit their
roles there to build a network
of Berlin-based designers and
manufacturers. "We started with
a website that included a shop
and a landing page for each
designer," says Soldo. "It was
important to tell the story of the
work." You can now peruse the
city's best design wares at the
permanent space in the charming
Bergmannkiez neighbourhood.
23 Nostitzstrasse, 10961
+49 (0)30 6800 8975
ofberlin.com

Homeware
House specials

①
Süper Store, Kreuzberg
Merchant tales

"We founded Süper to feature special craftsmanship" says Elisabeth Schotte, who set up the beguiling boutique in 2011 with Vanessa Marangoni. Since then the pair have drawn on previous careers in fashion design, furniture and antiques to seek out and showcase high-quality homeware, jewellery and stationery.

"We sell objects we believe have a story to tell and interesting craftsmen behind them," says Schotte. From Japanese bottle openers to Swiss paper products, expect an international ensemble of hard-to-come-by design pieces.
12 Dieffenbachstrasse, 10967
+49 (0)30 9832 7944
sueper-store.de

Minimum, Kreuzberg
Smart simplicity

As its name suggests, streamlined functionality takes centre-stage at this expansive yet homely showroom. Though the brand has three outposts across the city (Charlottenburg and Mitte being the other two), the Kreuzberg space caters to more modern tastes, from colourful shelving units by USM to plush Hay sofas and tableware in soft pastel tones. You'll find ample goods from homegrown talent here, including furniture by Berlin's Studio Alex Valder, sat alongside Minimum's own range of officeware.
85C Prinzenstrasse, 10969
+49 (0)30 7009 6260
minimum.de

Naturally, I shop at Minimum too

③
Room Capacity, Mitte
Objects of obsession

A mutual love of collecting art led Parisian chef Thomas Storai and Berlin businessman Jörn Kuschinsky to drop their careers and pursue their passion instead. "We wanted to create interiors with storied objects for like-minded eccentrics," says Kuschinsky.

The offering is mainly late 20th century and reflects the gritty charm of the showroom's location, which was a politically charged and quite rundown area after the Cold War. On show are Russian vintage prints, Italian lamps by iGuzzini, and restored pieces of unknown origin.
150 Linienstrasse, 10115
+49 (0)30 3385 1679
roomcapacity.de

Stilspiel, Kreuzberg
Treasure chest

Evelyn Lang and her partner Malte Henkel have been running this vintage-furniture shop for more than a decade now. The pair traverse the fairs, flea markets and dusty storerooms of Europe to find original art deco, Bauhaus and mid-century pieces from such designers as Charles Eames, Hans J Wegner and Wilhelm Wagenfeld.

The lamps, desks, chairs and tables only enter the Kreuzberg showroom after careful restoration – and if there's a certain something you're after, Lang or Henkel will enjoy the challenge of finding it.
95 Manteuffelstrasse, 10997
+49 (0)30 6040 2858
stilspiel.de

④
Halllesches Haus, Kreuzberg
Pull up a chair

"We wanted to create a convivial space, which we felt was missing in Berlin," says Hallesches Haus co-founder Oliver Cayless. "Somewhere you can shop, eat, or just have a coffee, all in one space." Cayless, Jillian May and Michelle Casciolo have achieved just that, restoring a red-brick, former nightclub into a lofty, light-filled space with high ceilings and vaulted archways.

A mix of practical and fanciful household items occupy the shelves, including Iris Hantverk brushes, Fundamental Berlin bowls and Paper Collective prints.
1 Tempelhofer Ufer, 10961
hallescheshaus.com

Clara Stil, Mitte
One for young and old

There's no shortage of design shops in Mitte but Clara Stil's refined stock of classic and contemporary furniture, lights and soft furnishings is always fresh. There's an emphasis on Nordic and German design, from promising Danish M/AU Studio to 125-year-old German furniture-maker Böwer. Also well represented is the city's new generation of design studios and creators, such as Studio Hausen, a shelf-builder that occupies the former ballroom of an old factory.
19 Rosa-Luxemburg-Strasse, 10178
+49 (0)30 2408 5014
clarastil.de

Specialist retail
Nice and niche

①
RSVP, Mitte
Stationery targets

The two outposts of stationer
RSVP sit opposite each other on
Mitte's Mulackstrasse. The original
2001 space stocks everything from
Italian leather-bound notebooks
and Kaweco and Caran d'Ache
pens to greeting cards from Berlin's
Marin Z Schröder. "Most of our
products are from small companies
or one-person-workshops, designers
and artists," says founder Meike
Wander (*pictured*).

The newer shop, designed by
Greek architect Manolis Iliakis,
has a wall dedicated to delightful
wrapping paper and ribbons.
14 & 26 Mulackstrasse, 10119
+49 (0)30 2809 4644
rsvp-berlin.de

②
Glasklar, Charlottenburg
Glass act

Glasklar has sold glassware in
Berlin since 1984. Monika Krause,
who took over the shop in 2012,
says it best: "Our concept is crystal
clear: we only sell clear glass."

The shop has a museum-like
seriousness. Shelves of glass and
wood line the walls, lit to bring
out the curves and edges of the
products. Stock ranges from
classics such as the Duralex
Picardie to the standard bearers
of German glass manufacturing,
Stölzle and Nachtmann.

Krause also pursues the more
unusual producers, exemplified by
mouth-blown glasses from Austrian
company Zalto, now in its seventh
generation of family ownership.
"I'm researching everywhere;
I've found nice items just going
out for dinner," she says.
13 Knesebeckstrasse, 10623
+49 (0)30 313 1037
glasklarberlin.com

Vintage shops
————
01 Down by Retro, Neukölln
It's quality, not quantity, here.
189 Weserstrasse, 12045
02 Trash Schick, Friedrichshain
Just the place for Berlin grunge.
trashschick.de
03 Chrome Store, Neukölln
High-end designer vintage.
chrome-store.com

④
Vintage Velo, Friedrichshain
Upcycled cycles

Just off a leafy square, Vintage Velo opened in 2015 and sources and refurbishes exemplary two-wheelers. Mathias Henfling serves "two kinds of customers: people who want fast bikes and the collectors. But in the end it is about passion."

While anyone can make a statement with a brand new, technologically advanced bike, Vintage Velo offers unique cycles worthy of conversation and envy. Italian and French frames in 1970s oranges and teals or 1990s neons are respectfully kept original.
2 Petersburger Platz, 10249
+49 (0)162 108 4887
vintageveloberlin.de

⑤
Jünemann's Pantoffeleck, Mitte
Class slippers

The Jünemann family has been making slippers in Mitte since 1908; their shop has occupied its current location since 1983, so its wooden shelves and rear workroom are worn to a cosy patina. The felt footwear is still handmade according to processes and designs that remain much unchanged.

Slippers come in a range of styles and colours including a signature brown check finished with felt or gum soles. Many Berliners buy multiple pairs to offer their houseguests at the door.
39 Torstrasse, 10119
+49 (0)30 442 5337
pantoffeleck.de

③
Paper & Tea, Charlottenburg
Enthusiasm for infusions

If anything could coerce members of Team Coffee to cross to Team Tea, it might be this place. The soft lighting, gallery-like displays and *gong fu* tasting tables are more like a love letter to tea than a retail outpost. Canadian-born founder Jens de Gruyter spent two years travelling and a further six months planning before opening the Charlottenburg concept shop in 2012. Highlights from his range of meticulously selected whole-leaf tea include Silver Sindano from Kenya, Mint Julep from Germany and Woori from Korea.
4 Bleibtreustrasse, 10623
+49 (0)30 555 798 071
paperandtea.com

⑥
Mykita, Mitte
Spectacle of it all

Eyewear label Mykita is a trailblazer when it comes to materials. From ultra-thin stainless steel to Italian acetates and the signature Mylon collection, made using 3D printing, each pair of specs is comfortable, dapper and made around the corner in Kreuzberg. Mykita's co-founder and creative director Moritz Krueger attributes keeping design and manufacturing under one Berlin roof to necessity rather than strategy. "The technology simply didn't exist to produce our first designs so we had to become our own manufacturer," he says.
6 Rosa-Luxemburg-Strasse, 10178
+49 (0)30 6730 8715
mykita.com

Books and records
Mixed media

2
Bücherbogen, Charlottenburg
Design tomes

Bücherbogen can be found in
Savignyplatz, one of the most
beautiful squares in the city, and
offers a slice of history. It's located
on the site of a former motor
workshop that specialised in
refabricating cars for refugees
fleeing from East Germany.

Bücherbogen originally
occupied one-and-a-half arches
under the main train line in
Charlottenburg; in 1980 it
expanded to five and in doing
so became one of the city's
largest bookshops dedicated to
architecture and design.
593 Stadtbahnbogen, 10623
+49 (0)30 3186 9511
buecherbogen-shop.de

1
Do You Read Me?!, Mitte
Primarily periodicals

In 2008 graphic designer Mark
Kiessling and bookseller Jessica
Reitz opened this small shop. It's
become a destination for anyone
seeking unusual periodicals; the
titles come from around the world
and are displayed on floor-to-ceiling
shelving and crowded tables.

The shop has a reading room on
Potsdamer Strasse for events and
often appears as a pop-up shop at
international fairs such as Design
Miami and Helsinki Design Week.
"They always say that print is about
to die," says Kiessling. "But our shop
is proof that that's not true at all."
28 Auguststrasse, 10117
+49 (0)30 6954 9695
doyoureadme.de

③

Soda, Mitte
Pick of the bunch

Sebastian Steinacker first opened Soda in Munich in 2004 and a decade later he expanded to Berlin. Together with his shop manager Isabell Hummel, Steinacker selects his favourite magazines and books from around the world and displays them in a crisp, uncluttered space. "We don't stack any publications on top of each other, which is one more reason for us to be picky about what we stock," says Hummel. Expect to find titles covering everything from typography to dogs, product design to gaming culture.
1 Weinbergsweg, 10119
+49 30 4373 3700
sodabooks.com

④

Pro QM Bookshop, Mitte
Urban survey

Pro QM seems less of a bookshop and more of a library owned by an absent-minded academic. But while there are no signs to direct you towards specific topics or genres (the stock is seemingly displayed at random), there is a system at work. Founded in 1999 by Katja Reichard, Jesko Fezer and Axel J Wieder, the shop has a thematic focus on Berlin: its politics, art, urban-planning, design and pop culture. It attracts architects, social scientists and creatives, both for the books and the programme of launches and presentations it hosts.
48 Almstadtstrasse, 10119
+49 (0)30 2472 8520
pro-qm.de

Obscure vinyl
—
Hard Wax is hard to locate and they probably like it that way; it's on the fourth floor of a run-down building at the back of a graffiti-stained apartment block. You won't find rock, pop or anything resembling chart music here – but you will uncover pure Berlin electro.
hardwax.com

⑤

Dodo Beach, Schöneberg
Vinyl frontier

Dodo Beach, which sits halfway down a quiet, unassuming street in residential Schöneberg, embraces all genres, which makes it a nice change for those tired of Berlin's electro offering. According to manager Stephan Schulz there are no restrictions on music category or style, just on quality. "In the tradition of independent record shops we don't say: 'We only sell punk or electro'. We stock everything we think is worth stocking." There's even a basement dedicated to heavy metal.
Dodo Beach was founded in 2013 and has swum against the tide of closing record shops and digital downloads to build a loyal fanbase of regular and international customers. Check the website for live events and release parties.
8 Vorbergstrasse, 10823
+49 (0)30 301 068 080
dodobeach.de

Four more bookshops

01 Dussmann, Mitte:
A plethora of books,
media, souvenirs and
stationery is housed across
this five-floored megastore
on Friedrichstrasse. Those
whose German is not up
to scratch should head
to the third floor where
more than 6,000
English-language titles
populate the shelves.
kulturkaufhaus.de

02 Saint George's English
Bookshop, Prenzlauer
Berg: The city's largest
selection of English-
language books is a
home away from home
for bibliophiles, not least
because Australian, US
and UK currencies are
accepted. New editions are
offered but secondhand
copies make up the bulk of
the stock. A significant
amount of shelf space is
given to works translated
from German.
saintgeorgesbookshop.com

03 Buchhandlung Walther
König, Mitte: This
international retailer and
publishing house emerged
from Köln's art scene in
the late 1960s. Its 14
shops can be found across
the city and are a safe
bet if you're after works on
architecture, contemporary
art and photography.
*buchhandlung-walther-
koenig.de*

04 Motto, Kreuzberg:
French-born photographer
Alexis Zavialoff founded
Motto as a distribution
company in 2007 and this
bookshop a year later.
"I stock only timeless
titles and some fanzines
– mostly about art, design
and fashion," he says.
Every few weeks there
are readings and there's
even a bar at the back.
mottodistribution.com

Department stores
Everything under one roof

①
Kadewe, Schöneberg
A German institution

There's no shortage of superlatives
to describe this 60,000 sq m retail
space. Kadewe (Kaufhaus des
Westens, literally "Department
Store of the West") is the place to
find luxury international brands
and German favourites.

The gourmet department on
the sixth floor is legendary. This
food temple is perfect for picking
up wurst and *weissbier* (wheat beer)
or having a nibble at one of the
gourmet bars and food counters. In
2018 its glass roof will be finished,
making for an extra-special dining
experience.
*21-24 Tauentzienstrasse, 10789
+49 (0)30 21 210
kadewe.de*

②
Departmentstore Quartier
206, Mitte
Home of the high-end

"I had a precise idea of my ideal
shopping destination and travelled
around the world for months to
buy all of the products for my
department store," says owner
Anne Maria Jagdfeld, who opened
Departmentstore Quartier 206
in 1997. The pointy building was
designed by New York architects
Pei Cobb Freed & Partners and
built between 1992 and 1995
in line with government plans
to resuscitate what was prewar
Berlin's main shopping street.

Beneath the star-shaped skylight
you'll find high-end international
fashion along with cosmetics,
books, flowers and homeware.
A few times a year you can also
participate in made-to-measure
appointments with some of the
shop's esteemed partners.
*71 Friedrichstrasse, 10117
+49 (0)30 2094 6500
quartier206.com*

*I came here
to shop but
I haven't
made it past
the food court*

Flea markets
Bargain hunt

dead of winter both are welcome. This is a tranquil counterpoint to the wild chaos of the nearby Mauerpark flea market.
Arkonaplatz
+49 (0)30 786 9764
troedelmarkt-arkonaplatz.de

① Trödelmarkt Fehrbelliner Platz, Wilmersdorf
Antiques galore

The dignified western suburb of Wilmersdorf is the home of Trödelmarkt Fehrbelliner Platz. It's a market that caters more to antiques hunters than fans of modern design, though a few local crafters and the option for anyone to rent a stall give some quotidian variation.

The backdrop is dramatic too: the platz is edged with some of the city's best-preserved examples of the controversial National Socialist architecture.
Fehrbelliner Platz
+49 (0)30 2435 8510
fehrbi.info

② Trödelmarkt Arkonaplatz, Mitte
Secondhand specials

This small market specialises in mid-century modern bric-a-brac and furnishings. From East German Ossi chic to classics such as Kaiser Idell lamps and teak tables, a stop here will smarten up any flat. Those in the know go early and get friendly with the dealers who come weekly.

There's a cart serving sausages and not-so-great coffee but in the

③ Flohmarkt am Mauerpark, Brunnenviertel
Trash and treasure

This expansive market requires a lot of sifting but it rewards the patient. Vintage German glassware and export china sit in rummage bins alongside jumbled detritus. Stalls specialising in batteries or bike parts are interspersed with those selling local crafts. Turkish food, currywurst and fresh-squeezed juices fuel browsing.

Alongside the market an amphitheatre with audience-participation karaoke makes for a raucous scene. There's something anarchic about the whole spectacle; it feels as if anything and everything might happen, from would-be virtuosos belting out Schlager hits and David Bowie to a communal Sia sing-along.
Mauerpark
+49 (0)30 2977 2486
flohnarktimmauerpark.de

Things we'd buy
—— Shop talk

In a city where creativity is encouraged and ingenuity celebrated, it shouldn't be a surprise that Berlin's retail scene is so varied and exciting.

But when you're faced with such a mind-boggling array of goods, how do you choose what to take home without lashing out on extra suitcases to carry it all? Do you sacrifice that jacket by the up-and-coming Berlin designer so you can pack the slippers from the company that's been making them since 1908? Can you get away with ditching the sauerkraut to make room for the artisan chocolate? Don't worry: with our shopping list you can have it all and more besides.

01 Knitwear by Wolfen
wolfengermany.com
02 Tea and thermos
by Paper & Tea
paperandtea.com
03 KPM x Minimum vases
from Minimum *minimum.de*
04 Beer and glass by
Hops & Barley
hopsandbarley-berlin.de
05 Sauerkraut from Kadewe
kadewe.de
06 Wooden bowl set
by Buchholz Berlin
buchholzberlin.com
07 Blutwurstmanufaktur sausage
from Kadewe
kadewe.de
08 Voo x Playtype cups
from Voo Store *vooberlin.com*
09 Van Nahmen apple juice
from Grünberger Weinhandlung
gruenberger-weinhandlung.de
10 Small Big Brands Lufthansa
cocktail mix from Of/Berlin
ofberlin.com
11 Berliner Brandstifter gin
from Kadewe
kadewe.de
12 Wooden chopping board
by Buchholz Berlin
buchholzberlin.com
13 Sausage from Kadewe
kadewe.de
14 Chocolate by Erich Hamann
hamann-schokolade.de
15 Tote by Do You Read Me?!
doyoureadme.de
16 Menswear by AD Deertz
addeertz.com
17 Vintage lettering from
Kartique *kartique.de*
18 Desk organiser
by Bartmann Berlin
bartmannberlin.de
19 Reality Studio shoes
from Voo Store *vooberlin.com*

20 Koch glassware from Of/Berlin
ofberlin.com
21 PB 0110 bag from
Andreas Murkudis
andreasmurkudis.com
22 Stationery from RSVP
rsvp-berlin.de
23 Eyewear by Mykita
mykita.com
24 *Berlin: Imagine a City* by
Rory MacLean from Bücherbogen
buecherbogen-shop.de

25 Nomos x Studio Mark Braun
watches from Leicht
leicht-jewellery.com
26 Slippers by Jünemann's
Pantoffeleck
pantoffeleck.de
27 Uslu Airlines cosmetics
from Kadewe
kadewe.de
28 *Freunde von Freunden:
Berlin* from Do You Read Me?!
doyoureadme.de

29 Frau Tonis Parfum Berlin
from Of/Berlin
ofberlin.com
30 Fundamental Berlin print
from Minimum
minimum.de
31 Vladimir Karaleev earrings
from Baerck
baerck.net
32 Fountain of Youth T-shirt
from Michelberger Hotel
michelbergermonkey.com

12 essays
—— Getting a
read on Berlin

❶
Downfall and rise
From suffering to stronghold
by Joseph Pearson,
writer

❷
Bike Berlin
Life on two wheels
by Rory MacLean,
writer

❸
Cities within cities
Berlin's urban development
by Jessica Bridger,
Monocle

❹
Go on, dive in
Freshwater swimming
by Robbie Lawrence,
photographer and writer

❺
West world
Life in the not-so-wild West
by Ole Schulz,
journalist

❻
Child of the East
Life in the GDR
by Elisabeth Rank,
writer

❼
Gathering's momentum
Berlin's subcultures
by Mikaela Aitken,
Monocle

❽
Rhythm of the night
Join the club
by Kati Krause,
Monocle

❾
Ein stein theory
Berlin beer culture
by Daniel Wighton,
writer

❿
What comes after
'poor but sexy'?
Culture in the city
by Kimberly Bradley,
Monocle

⓫
All aboard
Berlin's transport network
by Musa Okwonga,
journalist

⓬
Phoenix rising
Architecture in Berlin
by Marie-Sophie Schwarzer,
Monocle

*I really
need to
work on
my 'to-read'
pile...*

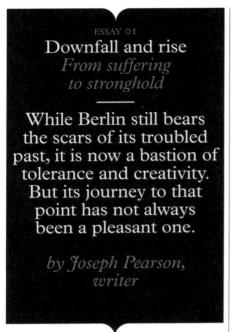

Downfall and rise
From suffering to stronghold

While Berlin still bears the scars of its troubled past, it is now a bastion of tolerance and creativity. But its journey to that point has not always been a pleasant one.

by Joseph Pearson, writer

Originally Berlin was known as Brlo, the "dry place in a swamp": an unlikely moniker for what would become one of Europe's greatest and most troublesome cities. By the 13th century it had become a market town; a bridge built over the Spree united it with the fellow trading post of Cölln but it was the Hohenzollern family – who ruled for 500 years from the 15th century – that truly engineered the city's meteoric rise.

As Berlin's lands expanded, so too did its military might. The Thirty Years' War (1618 to 1648) destroyed the city and convinced the then-insecure royals to invest in an oversized army. Prussia would eventually become known

as an "army with a state" and on a visit in 1764, diarist James Boswell discovered how soldiers were "beat like dogs" for the smallest transgression.

But focusing on military history only tells part of Berlin's story. Take Friedrich the Great, for example, who ruled from 1740 and was as passionate about his flute as he was his army; or the rise of Jewish intellectual life, as embodied by philosopher Moses Mendelssohn, whose grave can still be visited in the Old Jewish Cemetery; or the architectural achievements, such as Berlin's famed symbol the Brandenburg Gate, completed in 1791 and crowned by a goddess of peace.

The 19th century saw the defeat of Napoleon, the failure of the March 1848 revolution and the Unification of Germany in 1871. Industrial power soon followed and Berlin emerged as the continent's manufacturing hub, its population increasing significantly in 50 years.

While Wilhelm I worked towards a balance of power in Europe until his death in 1888,

---

Berlin bears

01 **Albert the Bear (died 1170):** Berlin was founded by the grandsons of this warlord who conquered the Slavs.
02 **Berlin's coat of arms:** The association of 'Bär' (bear) and 'Berlin' is phonetic.
03 **Knut (2006 to 2011):** Celebrity polar bear at Berlin Zoo.

his successor Wilhelm II – a compulsive tree-feller who almost certainly suffered from ADHD – took a more aggressive stance. In 1889 the Kaiser reportedly challenged touring US entertainer and exhibition shooter Annie Oakley to shoot off the end of his cigarette. During the First World War she asked if she might have another go.

The Great War buried a generation in the trenches those who did return were saddled with a victor's peace. Failed coups soon rocked the capital. Berliners lived in economic misery, forced to pay the cost of the war. During the 1923 hyperinflation, workers negotiated their wages by the hour; a suitcase was more valuable than all the money inside it.

"The Berlin Wall fell on 9 November 1989 and the land reunified on 3 October 1990. The new Germany was different: it had repented for its history"

A period of stabilisation did follow – with the artistic flourishing of expressionism, New Objectivity and Bauhaus – but the 1929 New York Stock Exchange crash again brought mass unemployment to the Weimar Republic. This crisis was the Nazis' chance to gain power and in 1933 Hitler became chancellor. Following a fire in the Reichstag that February he used emergency

powers to destroy Germany's first democracy. Political opponents were hunted down, the city became a fascist architectural project and minorities – the impaired, homosexuals, Roma and Jews – suffered violence at the hands of the state.

On 9 November 1938 the Night of Broken Glass, or *Kristallnacht,* saw vandalism of Jewish businesses and the destruction of most of Berlin's synagogues. The logistics for the Holocaust were later planned and directed from the German capital, epitomised by the infamous Wannsee Conference in January 1942. By war's end, 62,000 of the city's original 170,000 Jewish inhabitants had been killed, mostly in death camps.

In early 1943 the Nazis were defeated at Stalingrad and the Red Army marched towards Berlin, entering in April 1945. After being married for no more than 40 hours, Hitler and his bride Eva Braun killed themselves on 30 April. Everyday life for Berliners, meanwhile, was horrific: parts of the city, full of rats and rubble, were left in ruins by the war.

The victorious powers divided Berlin. The Western Zones – American, British, French – eventually became West Berlin, and the Soviet Eastern Zone became East Berlin. The Cold War was fought across the divided city; the Berlin Wall, built on 13 August 1961, and the site of many shootings along its "death strip", became a symbol of the division.

West Berlin enjoyed an Economic Miracle, or *Wirtschaftswunder*, fuelled by a multicultural workforce – notably Turkish workers who arrived from 1961. East Germany, meanwhile, enjoyed State protections but also restrictions on civil liberties. A sophisticated system of State surveillance, the Stasi, cast a shadow over private life.

In 1989 the USSR, transformed by Gorbachev's reforms and overstretched militarily, lifted its thumb from Eastern Europe. The Berlin Wall fell on 9 November 1989 and the land reunified on 3 October 1990. The new Germany was different from its predecessors: it had repented for its history. In 2015, 80,000 war refugees, mostly from the Middle East, were welcomed into the capital, a city that had known its fair share of authoritarianism and war. Berlin has emerged from its arduous history as an international byword for tolerance, creativity, sexiness and – most of all – resilience. — (M)

ABOUT THE WRITER: Joseph Pearson is the voice of *The Needle* blog and author of *Cityscapes Berlin* (Reaktion Books, 2017). With a history doctorate from Cambridge, he prefers long bike rides and nocturnal adventures to the archive.

ESSAY 02
Bike Berlin
Life on two wheels
────
Stretching from the open countryside into the heart of the capital and back again, the fall of the Wall left behind a trail that's just begging to be cycled.

by Rory MacLean, writer

We sliced through the woods on a straight path, our wheels wobbling in the sandy soil. Orderly ranks of trees fanned away in every direction, catching the light beneath their canopy and blocking out the blue sky. The forest trail dipped and crested but it didn't deviate from its linear course, stretching away to the west and toward a verdant vanishing point. On his leopard-spotted yellow bike – which was left abandoned in our apartment's courtyard by a departing neighbour – my seven-year-old son pulled ahead of me, lost his balance and then regained it. A month earlier he had hardly been able to ride. Now he stood up on his pedals and whooped. Like him, I was thrilled by the sense of freedom. I felt as if we could ride on out of Berlin, as far as Hamburg or Paris. "Daddy, let's ride to the ends of the Earth!" he shouted.

Suddenly the trail changed direction. A neat, new paved cycle lane cut across our path, curving away to the north and south. Beyond it stretched empty fields. Yet despite the open vista, the sense of freedom left me, either because of something latent in the air or because of my knowledge of the history of this place. Above us, a sign read Berliner Mauerweg.

In 1961 communist East Germany built the Wall to stop its citizens escaping to the capitalist West (3.5 million East Germans had fled their country over the previous 15 years). The reinforced concrete barrier, with its guard towers, anti-vehicle trenches and "death strip" completely encircled the western half of the city. After the Wall fell, the 160km-long Berlin Wall Trail was established along the route of the former border fortifications, cutting through the countryside and into the heart of the reunified city. It runs by the Reichstag and Brandenburg Gate, past Checkpoint Charlie and Friedrichstrasse S-Bahn station (once the only rail-crossing point between the two halves of the city) and the so-called Tränenpalast (Palace of Tears) where countless farewells took place before 1989.

All my life I've been besotted with cycling. Time and again my bicycle has freed me, giving me a sense of both belonging and independence. In Berlin it has enabled me to know the city as well as – if not better – than many of its residents. I like the fact that cyclists can never be passive passengers. Each ride is proof of our corporeal existence and of our ability to control our movement through space.

For me a ride along the Mauerweg brings great happiness – and not just because one can go for hours without meeting another soul on its rural sections. Rather it was here, along this old border, that the decades of totalitarianism – first under fascism and then under communism – seemed to have been swept out of Europe.

The Wall Trail is divided into 14 sections that vary between 7km and 21km in length; bicycles can be rented at hundreds of outlets. Along the route there are more than 40 information points that offer details on the division and reunification of Germany, as well as on the construction and fall of the Wall. Images and texts describe events that happened at the sites, such as the story of the farmer who broke through the Wall in his tractor to help to reunite the divided city.

> "I like the fact that cyclists can never be passive passengers. Each ride is proof of our corporeal existence"

My son and I often ride along the Mauerweg, cycling between the once-separated suburbs and villages of Spandau and Staaken, Falkensee and Siedlung Schönwalde. As the sun flickers through the trees he sings to himself, then stands on his pedals and whoops again. The Wall does not exist for him, of course, but then neither do the divisive nationalism and romantic pretensions that increasingly threaten the European dream. In his mind he will always be free to ride as far as Hamburg, Paris, even London – and to the ends of the Earth. — (M)

ABOUT THE WRITER: Rory MacLean is one of Britain's most expressive and adventurous travel writers. His 12 books include the UK top 10's *Stalin's Nose*, as well as *Under the Dragon* and *Berlin: Imagine a City*. His works, wrote the late John Fowles, are among those that marvellously explain why literature still lives. A fellow of the Royal Society of Literature, he divides his time between Berlin, London and Dorset.

Berlin cyclists

01 Tilda Swinton
The actress circled the Wall in 1988 short 'Cycling the Frame'.
02 David Bowie
The Thin White Duke often rode out to Hansa Studios.
03 Franz Kafka
The author felt 'the bracing effect of Berlin' while astride a 1920s two-wheeler.

ESSAY 03
Cities within cities
Berlin's urban development

——

Berlin is a collection of mini cities with unique personalities. And their preservation is down to both urban planners and the ravages of war.

*by Jessica Bridger,
Monocle*

Berlin has many centres and can be seen as a collection of smaller, individual cities. True, other metropolises have distinct neighbourhoods – such as Wan Chai and Kennedy Town in Hong Kong, or the South End and Roxbury in Boston – but usually these neighbourhoods pull towards a singular centre. In Berlin each 'hood exists almost autonomously and has its own identity.

Since the 1940s the city has been slowly reconstituted from the destruction wrought in the Second World War. Bombing raids destroyed great swathes of the city. Haunting photographs of the era show vast landscapes where only pavements and kerbstones remained after the rubble and damaged buildings were cleared away. The ensuing political tug of war, first between the occupying powers and then between East and West Germany, made urban development equal parts impossible and competitive.

Berlin's island-like neighbourhoods and history of destruction have inspired ecologists and urban-design theorists. One key project was the 1957 International Building Exhibition (IBA), which saw architects such as Alvar Aalto and Oscar Niemeyer revitalise the neighbourhood of Hansaviertel (*see page 107*) at the edge of Tiergarten in West Berlin.

The city was at the forefront of urban ecology in the 1970s. Ecologists studied empty lots where new habitats were created and wildlife uniquely suited to urban life was flourishing. This ecological aspect of Berlin's urban development is still visible today at Südgelände, a nature reserve in the south of

**Public transit lines
from which to witness the
city's many centres**

01 **Tram M5:** Hackescher Markt to Lichtenberg and Malchow. 02 **S-Bahn Line 1:** From Wannsee's lakes to Potsdamer Platz, Wedding and Frohnau. 03 **Bus 100:** From Zoologischer Garten and Tiergarten to Alexanderplatz.

the city. Here vegetation grows between the old railway lines and a network of paths crisscross the manmade forest.

Architect OM Ungers published a now-canonical manifesto in 1977 called *Berlin: A Green Archipelago*. He suggested keeping buildings in concentrated areas while letting other parts run wild, creating a new kind of planned urban paradise. The postwar population decline, wartime clearance and pre-defined, autonomous districts helped to enable this romantic idea.

> "The wild, rambling lots are gone. Buildings have been slotted into place like expensive dental work"

It would be wrong to attribute the individual characteristics of each mini-city solely to postwar redevelopment. As it expanded, Berlin slowly swallowed up smaller cities, many of which were already established. For example, Köpenick in the southeast lies next to the large Müggelsee and was only incorporated into the city in the 1920s. It has the dreamy feel of a lakeside town and its residents are proud of their independent nature. You could spend a lifetime in Köpenick, rarely leave and have that become "your" Berlin.

In recent decades Berlin has entered a phase of fevered gap-filling. When I first came here in 2008, I could still find vacant plots with small jungles of knotweed and ailanthus trees at major intersections throughout Mitte. Now those wild, rambling lots are gone. Buildings have been slotted into place like expensive dental work. Large fields of green have been swallowed or tamed into parks.

One of the last big green spaces designed to stitch the city together was Park am Gleisdreieck (*see page 124*), completed in 2013. On the site of a former railyard in the centre of the city, its smart design includes playgrounds and other public spaces that unite the communities of the Bergmannkiez neighbourhood and Schöneberg's rougher eastern edge.

At times, these varying versions of Berlin can be too extreme in their differences to knit together. Although some of the smaller hubs such as Mitte and Prenzlauer Berg are now almost indistinguishable, others will never lose their distinct traits.

Lichtenberg is certainly not the Berlin that you associate with glossy travel articles. Here highway-wide roads traverse open fields dotted with tower blocks. Circus tents and drive-through restaurants beckon. In the postwar period large parts of the neighbourhood were developed into communal-housing projects. Immigrant workers, many from Turkey and Vietnam, were given accommodation here en masse, in turn leading to the formation of ethnic enclaves.

Today the Dong Xuan Center wholesale market in Lichtenberg is the place to go for a taste of Vietnamese-influenced Berlin – and the city's best roasted-pork soup. Head to the canalside border of Kreuzberg and Neukölln and you'll find a weekly Turkish market that offers fresh produce best perused with a cheese-stuffed gözleme flatbread in hand.

Made up of myriad pockets drawn together and split apart by historical forces, Berlin is bursting with different flavours. It's also, as a result, a wonderful place to explore: why choose one city when you can have multiple mini ones? — (M)

ABOUT THE WRITER: Jessica Bridger is a contributing editor for MONOCLE. She works as a journalist, consultant and urbanist. Her consultancy conducts expert research, strategic planning and communications projects for public and private-sector clients.

ESSAY 04

Go on, dive in
Freshwater swimming
────

There's no need to leave the city if you're hankering for escape: Berlin has many lakes where you can swim, enjoy nature and relax.

by Robbie Lawrence, photographer and writer

I moved to Berlin a couple of years ago, arriving in early autumn. Having endured a typically brutal winter – a period when one's primary outdoor activity is a quick shuffle to the nearest U-Bahn station, collar raised against sleet and driving winds – I felt unadulterated joy as the days began to lengthen in late April. It was around this time that I discovered the pleasures of exploring the capital's lakes.

I grew up in blustery Edinburgh – a city both mountainous and coastal – spoilt by easy access to the windswept beaches of Tyninghame and the vertiginous slopes of Arthur's Seat. Prior to moving to landlocked Berlin I had associated the city with its tumultuous history, iconic concrete skyline, beer gardens and galleries but knew little of its natural beauty. As spring unfurled I began to explore the grandeur of Tiergarten, the great grassy sprawl of Tempelhofer Feld (*see page 125*) and the gentle inclines of Viktoriapark. However, it was only when a friend and I cycled to Plötzensee for an afternoon dip that I discovered the true extent of the city's open-air offerings.

The spring light, dimmed by the foliage above, cast filmy rays upon the vista, outlining the pale silhouettes of naked figures as they dipped beneath the water. Birds chirped, newspaper pages fluttered in the light breeze and barbecue smoke hung in the air. This was not a bucolic retreat in the countryside but a 10-minute walk from the autobahn in Moabit. In search of a grassy knoll where we could drop our towels we passed a boat-hire company, where couples sipped beers and rowed lazily through the reeds. On the opposite bank children played on the manmade beach. As I broke the surface of the water I sensed the familiar thrill of being alone in nature. I struck out to the middle of the lake, where the water began to cool and voices from the banks faded.

Now I get out to the lakes as much as possible. I am spoilt for choice: the state of Brandenburg is said to have more than 3,000 and about 100 of these fall within the city limits. My particular favourite is Gross Glienicker See, a relatively quiet lake in the southwest on the edge of Potsdam. Not only is the water there particularly clear but it is home to two leafy islands where bathers rest after an arduous swim. Its northern bank is the ideal vantage point to watch the sunset. I now spend many evenings there, either reading or picnicking with friends as the

rusty summer light dips below the treeline. Other lakes worthy of a mention are Templiner See, known for its sailing; the peaceful and secluded Habermannsee, with its unkempt reedy banks; and the vast Liepnitzsee, where one can swim and trek. If you are reading this with your tickets to Berlin booked for autumn or winter, don't despair. My initial assumption that people avoided the lakes during the colder months was proven wrong when I watched an old chap take a plunge in December with nothing to protect him but a thick rug of back hair and a Santa hat.

Jessica J Lee is the author of Berlin wild-swimming memoir *Turning*. She set herself the challenge of swimming in a different lake every week for one year, an admirable feat. "When you swim out into the middle of the lake there's that feeling of being *right* in the middle, the world moving around you and you're suspended by water," says Lee. "Because so much of Berlin and Brandenburg is taken up by water, swimming is a natural way in." Indeed, if you're willing to join the ranks of naked Germans, wurst in one hand, stein in the other, then a venture to the lakes will give you an insight into one of the many reasons that locals are so fond of this great city. — (M)

> *"I watched an old chap take a plunge in December with nothing to protect him but a thick rug of back hair and a Santa hat"*

Right lake for the right occasion

01 Gross Glienicker See
This is perfect for a romantic date night.
02 Schlachtensee
To be enjoyed with sausages, beer and good friends.
03 Mühlenbecker See
Hit up this lake for a rugged swim.

ⓘ

ABOUT THE WRITER: Robbie Lawrence is a Scottish photographer and writer. In 2013 he worked as features editor of *Cereal* magazine. In late 2014 he moved to Berlin to take up the head of photography position at *Freunde von Freunden* and, after an exhilarating year, decided to take the next step and go freelance.

ESSAY 05

West world
Life in the not-so-wild West

The old West was isolated but that didn't mean that life there was miserable. One writer tells of what it was like to come of age on the 'free' side of the fence.

*by Ole Schulz,
journalist*

Best of the West

01 Siegessäule
Climb its 285 steps and look over both sides of the city.
02 Winterfeldtmarkt
The farmers' market is a Schöneberg institution.
03 Freibad Plötzensee
A beach resort around a natural lake in Wedding that provides a calm place to relax.

If somebody asks me who I am, I tell them I am a man from the last century – and a child of the Wall.

When I was born in West Berlin in 1968 the Wall had been standing for seven years. People often forget that it wasn't just Berlin that was divided in two but the whole of Germany, and this Wall encircled my hometown completely.

I don't want to give you the wrong impression: we didn't feel imprisoned or incarcerated – we were used to it. And life in the so-called "showcase of the West" had its advantages. It was a green city, with plenty of lakes, public pools and bathing spots, parks and woods. I grew up in Tiergarten near the large city park so the Wall was all the way on the other bank of the Spree, behind the abandoned Reichstag. Sometimes we would go just to peer at the other side but, to be honest, we weren't really all that interested in East Berlin. If I think about it today, I can't believe how ignorant we were.

The 1970s and 1980s were a great time to be a child in West Berlin. Our parents earned more money than people in other parts of West Germany because they received *Berlinzulage*, a kind of bonus due to the lack of manpower in the city. Most could afford to live in large, cheap apartments with stucco ceilings and tremendous swing doors. A number of young outsiders, libertines and artists from West Germany migrated to Berlin to avoid mandatory army service. Bomb craters left by the Second World War were used as green spaces and abandoned buildings were squatted or used for cultural projects. And we had another luxury: no curfew, unlike other West Geman cities.

Again, I may be painting a slightly skewed picture. West Berlin wasn't really cosmopolitan. We led a quiet existence and shared the city with no more than two million people. Kreuzberg nights may have been long – as Gebrüder Blattschuss's 1978 song suggests – and the cultural underground was alive with punks, mods, goths and hippies, but subculture as a lifestyle was not as pronounced as it is today. I used to think I was a city slicker but now I realise that wasn't the case.

Whenever we wanted to leave the city we had to pass through one of four transit highways to the other states in the Federal Republic of Germany. The first border was at the city limits, where the grim looking *Grenzpolizisten* (GDR border policemen) would stop you and search your car on a whim. One day they confiscated the best part of my comic-book collection, claiming it was capitalist propaganda. My parents were convinced that the guards just wanted something entertaining to read.

It was often said that East Berlin was grey and a strong smell of coal hung in the air during winter. But it wasn't so different in the West. Like the East we had our fair share of empty and dilapidated buildings. This saw a wave of squatters settle in Kreuzberg and Schöneberg in the early 1980s. When I left my parents' home the first flat I moved to only had stove heating; there was no hot water and the toilet was in the hallway. I laugh when I look back at my old photos: I had long hair, stone-washed jeans and a plush pullover that always bore a sticker with a slogan such as: "Stop nuclear power!"

I turned 20 in 1988. It was a rebellious time and I flitted from demonstration to demonstration, whether against nuclear weapons, Ronald Reagan or the ruling conservative party CDU. As a young member of the left I was against the "system" and dreamed about a better society.

"We didn't feel imprisoned or incarcerated – we were used to it. And life in the West had its advantages"

It wasn't easy to justify the existence of the Anti-Fascist Protective Wall, as the GDR government dubbed the Wall. But the GDR had been the only real existing alternative to capitalism, which we condemned as well.

Then suddenly, on 9 November 1989, the Wall came down. We were totally surprised by it. How marvellous it was to experience a revolution firsthand and in my twenties. Admittedly though, it was hard for us to comprehend what the fall of the Wall and the collapse of the Eastern bloc meant. It took me years to realise and accept that I was raised in a special era that was never going to last forever.

Since the turn of the century a large number of Berlin's inner-city districts have undergone gentrification. Lately I've started to discover the calm of the more traditional neighbourhoods of West Berlin. Some remain exactly as I remember: there's a small grocer's on the corner, a bakery and a public square with some trees and nothing more. I would never wish to have the Wall back but I do sometimes miss the laidback atmosphere of my childhood in the West. — (M)

ABOUT THE WRITER: Ole Schulz is a historian and journalist from west Berlin. He works across print, online and public radio, covering stories on Berlin and Latin America. Returning from Latin America's big cities, he realises what a liveable place Berlin still is.

ESSAY 06

Child of the East
Life in the GDR

With personal freedoms strictly policed and constant surveillance a fact of daily life, growing up in totalitarian East Berlin was no easy feat. Yet for this writer it felt – and still feels – like home.

by Elisabeth Rank, writer

"It felt unnerving to watch people taking pictures of themselves with the Wall at their backs, until I took one too"

Some say it's a feeling, others that it's the people who surround you but to me, home is that one view from the car window.

When I was a kid, my family often travelled to the Baltic Sea during summer. On the return journey, 10 minutes before you could make out the details of the city, you could see the TV Tower. It appeared on the horizon and looked like an apple plunged onto a stick but to me it said one thing: home.

It was the same for many others who lived in the East. The TV Tower was built to provide broadcasting services but also became a cherished landmark. I grew up just a few blocks away, in the centre of town. Recently my grandpa, who worked as a photographer, showed me a picture of the tower while it was still under construction. He took it sometime between 1965 and 1969 – from the very top. To get the shot he had to lie down while a friend sat on his legs to stop him from falling. They weren't allowed up there but there

they were, atop the unfinished tower. That's what people did back then: they found ways to overcome the rules of a totalitarian state.

It was the same with education: only a few people were allowed to get a university entrance diploma. My mum, aunt and uncle were not among those chosen. They weren't able to seek tertiary education because my grandma had worked as a doctor and one doctor per family was deemed enough.

My family tried to live by different rules. Some of my relatives tried to escape the GDR; some failed while others made it to the West. As a result we lived with permanent surveillance. I remember the two men who were waiting in front of our house every morning as my mum and I left for nursery. I often waved hello because I was so used to their presence. They followed us as we walked up the hill and around the corner. By the time I entered nursery and peered back, they were gone.

But someone was always watching. Even in nursery we were not allowed to pick the people or the toys that we played with. One day I refused to eat my apple. The staff called my mum and told her that I was a revolutionist and that she should be wary. My mum then told me that she was proud of me for standing up for myself and that she had taken the blame. Unfortunately it was too late, I was labelled a rebel – and the teachers had formulated their own punishments for children who opposed their authority.

I was fast asleep on 9 November 1989 when my dad, who worked as a cook, heard the news and went to the Wall, which was just 400 metres from our house. He saw it fall. I remember waking up the next morning and seeing the euphoric expression on his face. I didn't understand what he meant when he spoke of freedom and the right to travel: I was five years old. Now I know.

Whenever I pass by Bernauer Strasse I remember my dad's jubilant face. There's now a memorial there for people who were shot trying to escape the GDR. I recommend you visit the information centre to see the pieces of the Wall that are still standing. It was strange to visit because to me it was a place for soldiers, not tourists; it felt unnerving to watch people taking pictures of themselves with the Wall at their backs, until I took one too. I reclaimed that place with a smile and a sense of nostalgia.

The first thing people say when they hear that I'm from Berlin and that I still live there is, "Oh, you're one of the few." They normally follow with, "Don't you miss the old Berlin?" It's at this moment that I remember my grandpa's old photos and the grey houses covered in rough plaster that populate the images. It wasn't just the houses that used to be grey: everything was. After the Wall fell the grey faded – and today I am happy to be surrounded by colour. — (M)

Discover the Berlin wall

01 Visitor Center at Bernauer Strasse
Original pieces of the Wall.
02 Mauerweg
Bike along the 160km-long path where the Wall was located.
03 Berlin-Hohenschönhausen memorial
Old Soviet prison.

ABOUT THE WRITER: Elisabeth Rank lives in Berlin and works at *Zeitmagazin*. In 2010 she published a novel, *Und im Zweifel Für Dich Selbst (And in Doubt for Yourself)*, and a second in 2013 titled *Bist du Noch Wach? (Are You Still Awake?)*. Her blog is at *lisarank.de*.

ESSAY 07
Gathering's momentum
Berlin subcultures

Berlin's cultural forces are about much more than partying: over the years they've been the embodiment of self-expression, political non-conformity and social evolution.

by Mikaela Aitken, Monocle

Berlin has a reputation for revelry. But it would be a mistake to dismiss this penchant for partying as merely a love of getting loose: late-night socialising has a storied past in Berlin – and has had a weighty cultural impact too. Through its crowded cabaret clubs and grimy punk venues, a rollcall of unconventional characters and evolving subcultures have long contributed to the fabric of this peculiar city.

It took a few decades for the aristocratic salons of Paris to reach Berlin. However, by the early 1800s, educated women were wise to their French counterparts' method of bypassing housewifely duties. Daughters of Jewish aristocrats started to invite Berlin's most inquisitive minds – plus those with the deepest pockets (and therefore the most social cache) – around for dinner.

Whom a *salonnière* was able to lure into her living room depended on her charm and wit. It was a 19th-century flourish in feminism, where salon owners were key in connecting the businessman to the artist and the philanthropist. Conversations were free from high-society pretentions and ripe with optimism, cultural liberty and equality. The salon subculture and its intellectual evenings awoke the liberal-arts movement in Berlin.

The debauchery of cabaret soon followed. While sitting in a room with revolutionary minds and musical protégés was rather swell, the city's creative community hungered for wanton lust and dazzling extravagance. This, coupled with a rather lax police commissioner in the 1890s, allowed the gay community to flourish. Homoeroticism surfaced as a prominent subculture and a range of bawdy events including Damenklub Altes Geld (Old Money Ladies Club) and Böse-Buben Balle (Bad Boy Balls) filled the social calendar.

Men with rouged cheeks and flowing lace frocks were emblems of the cabaret world. Husband and wife would regularly toddle to these small clubs, even throwing down a few extra coins for a private shimmy from their favourite dancer. Even though homosexuality was illegal, the public enjoyed increased liberties and by the Golden Twenties a growing portion of Berlin had achieved tolerance for the gay community. This new-found freedom, however, inexorably collided with the rise of Hitler and this subculture and the gay rights movement splintered.

The next notable rebellion to surface in Berlin was punk in the 1980s. Kids with torn jeans, chains and an affinity for frenetic music populated the tired streets of West Berlin. The isolated metropolis was a hotbed for anarchists and liberals skiving from West German military school. The city also attracted expats such as David Bowie, Iggy Pop, Nick Cave and Brian Eno and played host to visitors The Clash, Sex Pistols and Joy Division. Bands played haphazard gigs in Kreuzberg's abandoned apartments.

Mark Reeder, a Brit who was living in the walled city at the time and managing punk bands, sought to explore the scene on the other side of the divide. Travelling as a tourist, he crossed to the East and found a small punk community playing quick tempo tracks with leftist lyrics on homemade instruments. To avoid attracting Stasi attention, Reeder arranged for West Berlin-based band Die Toten Hosen to play a gig under the guise of a church performance. The priest had the bleach-haired punks agree to take part in the mass and prayers beforehand, emphasising they were, after all, playing a church service.

"The dance floors of the techno subculture worked to unite the youth of an estranged nation"

Several dozen East German fans braved the mass. From here, the East German punk subculture, under protection of the church, swelled. Eventually key figures would be arrested and sent to work camps – an attempt by the Stasi to stem the rebellion. But by then, love of punk was widespread. The Stasi changed tack and infiltrated the scene, offering bribes in return for pro-state rhetoric. In 1989 with the fall of the Wall – and their enemy – the punk crusade fell somewhat silent.

As the East opened up, young creatives streamed in to occupy the empty

Berlin techno acts

01 Pan-Pot
Techno house from the pairing of Thomas Benedix and Tassilo Ippenberger.
02 Modeselektor
Berlin duo plays blend of electro house and hip hop.
03 Apparat
AKA electronic musician Sascha Ring.

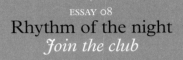
apartments. They explored the deserted GDR factories and ex-military buildings and began hosting illicit parties with thumping electronic music that rumbled through the expansive industrial spaces. Revellers included a mix of brazen West German squatters and East Germans discovering the pleasures of freedom.

In the early 1990s the premise for a lot of these raves was salacious fetishes but organisers eventually started to cater to a wider audience. Plaid shirts became just as welcome as leather chaps, as long as the techno trance played on. The unabashed strobe-laden dance floors of the techno subculture worked to unite the youth of an estranged nation.

Art critic Karl Scheffler witheringly wrote in 1910: "Berlin is a city condemned forever to becoming and never being." When considering the number and diversity of the subcultures the city has cycled through, there may be some truth to that. But to disparage the impact that these stages of cultural flux have had would also be false. Berliners have proven their ability to create social change, all while throwing some pretty impressive parties. And that's a fact to revel in. — (M)

ESSAY 08

Rhythm of the night
Join the club

While reports of its death have been greatly exaggerated, nightlife in the German capital is certainly changing. But there is one constant: the bouncers.

*by Kati Krause,
Monocle*

I don't go out partying much anymore. This might seem a strange confession at the start of an essay that claims to give its readers a sense of Berlin's nightlife but I make it with the confidence of someone who has the weight of trends behind her. Becasue *nobody* in Berlin goes out partying much anymore.

This development has been discussed at dinner parties, in bars and by both national and international media, and has led some – international commentators, mostly – to declare that Berlin is "over". The reason given is that gentrification has killed off the city's most libertarian corners and wildest clubs and that the nightlife these days is much better in Leipzig, Warsaw or Belgrade, any of which are the

ABOUT THE WRITER: Mikaela Aitken is assistant editor for MONOCLE's book series. While reporting for this guide she had every intention of researching the city's raucous industrial dance floors but responsibly chose to keep her 09.00 meetings instead.

"new Berlin". The debate reached fever pitch in 2014, the year that clubs Cookies and Kater Holzig (itself successor to the late Bar 25) closed and prompted *Mit Vergnügen* magazine to publish a widely shared response to the naysayers, titled: "Berlin isn't over. It's hungry." Its theory was that Berlin's nightlife wasn't changing because all the clubs had died (the Germans even have a word for the death of clubs: *clubsterben*). Instead it blamed fewer young people, a lack of musical innovation and (apparently) Berliners now being more interested in eating than dancing. "Markthalle Neun [*see page 39*] is the new Berghain," the magazine proclaimed.

They have a point. One of Berlin's most popular parties is the monthly Burgers & Hip Hop food fest at Prince Charles. The owners of Cookies and Bar 25 have turned their clubs into restaurants; the latter is part of a "creative village" that includes a childcare centre. Recently an asparagus festival in a Brandenburg village was cancelled in a panic after thousands of Berliners RSVP'd on Facebook. And in terms of currency, knowledge of the next unusual pop-up restaurant counts for a lot more than a guestlist contact for a private afterparty.

"Not going out much' can mean meeting friends for dinner at a chic restaurant and later finding yourself handing your trousers to the bouncers at KitKatClub"

Of course, we've all grown older – both the people who led Berlin's party heyday and those who followed them. What I used to love most about Berlin nightlife was that clubs are – or were – often found in repurposed buildings that allowed you to get utterly lost in them: Wilde Renate's multi-floor residential building, Berghain's power station or Stattbad Wedding's underground

> **Things that haven't changed in 25 years**
>
> **01 The state of the toilets**
> Relieving oneself continues to be a minority activity.
> **02 The state of the U-Bahn**
> Turns into a drinking spot on weekends after 22.00.
> **03 The music**
> Techno, techno, techno.

swimming pool, for example. What I love most about Berlin's nightlife now is that it also happens during the day: Berghain on a Sunday morning, Mauerpark on a Sunday afternoon or the many concerts and small parties that take place, often spontaneously, at train stations and cornershops. Yet when I asked my neighbour, a 23-year-old professional DJ who grew up in Mitte, where the kids party these days, he gave me a blank look and shrugged: "I don't like techno so I can't really say."

But before you get a false impression, the purported decline of Berlin nightlife should be given some context. "Not going out much" often means "not planning to go out much", which are two very different things. Berlin still has a powerful way of sucking you into its nightlife. Horror stories abound of Australian musicians who came to the city to boost their creativity and careers, only to disappear into a vortex of drugs and drink and be spat out again several months later, dishevelled, disoriented and scrambling to make their way back home. "Not going out much" can mean attending the annual graduation show at the University of the Arts in the early evening and somehow still being there at 06.00. It can mean going to swing night at Clärchens Ballhaus and ending up dancing at Bar 3 and wondering how to cancel your morning meeting without arousing suspicion. It can mean catching up with friends for dinner at a chic restaurant and later finding yourself handing your trousers to the bouncers at KitKatClub because… well, it's better you find that out for yourselves.

If there's one thing that has remained reassuringly constant about Berlin's nightlife, it's the bouncers. I remember a time when I was young and poor in a city that wasn't Berlin and the biggest challenge about clubbing was how to get in for free. Later, as I prowled Berlin with a wad of cash in my pocket, the biggest challenge was how to get in, period.

Being turned away at a club is jarring. That bored look just over your shoulder, the lazy "Sorry, not today" – it's hard not to take it as a personal rejection, especially because, unlike in other cities, the reason isn't usually your dress (unless you're wearing a football shirt). Famous musicians have gone on petulant social-media rants after being turned away at Berghain (which is not a good look). Once Caesar has lowered his thumb, all you can do is pretend to accept the verdict with grace: a shrug, maybe a joke, and a plan B. Because despite all the moans and groans about the decline of Berlin nightlife, you'll never be short of a plan B. — (M)

ESSAY 09

Ein stein theory
Berlin beer culture

——

It's known as a hub for beer drinkers yet brews created within the city itself are few and far between. But could it be that Berlin brewpubs will change all that?

*by Daniel Wighton,
writer*

ABOUT THE WRITER: Kati Krause grew up in Munich and lived in London and Barcelona for 10 years before moving to Berlin, where she is MONOCLE's correspondent. She has edited several print and online magazines and contributed to publications such as *Zeit Online*, the *Wall Street Journal*'s European edition and *Freunde von Freunden*.

For generations Germany has been known as the world's beer capital: the country still conjures images of glass boots filled with amber liquid, crusty salted pretzels and the hearty clinking of steins. It may come as a surprise then that the capital city of this capital of beers isn't all that capital when it comes to local brews. That doesn't mean Berlin is not a beer town; far from it. Like a 1700s Bavarian monk during lent, Berlin runs on the stuff.

But for such a liberal city, beer culture in Die Hauptstadt has remained notoriously conservative. Perhaps as a reaction to the turmoil of the 20th century, Berliners have been reluctant to change their beer-consumption habits. In recent decades much of the city has relied on larger industrial breweries rather than the centuries-old monasteries that have traditionally influenced brewing throughout the south and west of the country.

Unsatisfied with the local selection, Berliners have generally been happy to import their beer from elsewhere. Even today the enduring popularity of Czech beers across East Berlin is reflective of the historical difficulty of obtaining anything from the other side of the Iron Curtain. Without mentioning names, the informal rule adopted by many beer drinkers tends to be that if it has "Berlin" in the name, it is best avoided.

This disdain for the local brew means that, unlike most German cities where pride in regional beer still reigns supreme (and the options usually include the local lager, dark and wheat beers, some Beck's and not much else), in Berlin variety is the spice of life.

Berliners with a fondness for the bitter northern-German pilsner-style beers can

> *"A lack of restrictions has created a culture that supports self-policing"*

easily find varieties such as Jever and Flensburger, whereas those with a taste for the malty Bavarian-style lagers have no trouble getting their hands on Munich favourites such as Augustiner. Any self-respecting *späti* (late-night cornershop) or supermarket will also stock a range of wheat and dark beers. Even finding regional specialities such as kölsch (Köln) or altbier (Düsseldorf) is less difficult than it would be in other large German cities.

However, as has always been the case in Berlin, change is afoot. Over the past decade the options have proliferated for something previously thought impossible: good beer from Berlin.

Brewpubs and smaller breweries have begun to spring up in trendy and non-trendy neighbourhoods alike. And though traditionalists may still mumble the words through clenched teeth, "craft beer" is catching on.

While Germans have been doing craft beer since before it was cool (think Catholic monks producing batches of doppelbock in the 11th century) it's only recently that

What your toast says about you
——
01 Prost
Traditional, festive and fun; let the party begin.
02 Zum wohl
Literally 'to your health'. This one's for the hearty evenings.
03 Stösschen
For the more refined drinker. Pinkies out, please.

supply has begun to meet widespread demand. However, not all craft beers are created equal. Those looking to sample the local tipple should dig a little deeper, past the hip locales offering pale ales from the US for something *ein bisschen* more Berlin.

Brewpubs such as Hops & Barley in Friedrichshain (*see page 43*) and Eschenbräu in Wedding have some creative varieties but also offer modern twists on classic German staples (those who think craft beer begins and ends with pale ale will find something to tickle their fancy). Otherwise, for something you might not be able to get at home, try a helles or a dunkel.

Although Berlin's beer-brewing culture may have historically been lacking, don't make the mistake of equating that with beer-*drinking* culture, which is strictly top shelf. A complete lack of restrictions on alcohol – there is no legally required closing time for bars and clubs and drinking in the park or on the street is legal – has created a culture that supports self-policing. Berliners have schooled themselves in moderation. Bars will not hesitate to ask you to leave – or not let you in in the first place – if they feel you are abusing the privilege. Just never ask the bartender to serve your beer out of a glass boot. You've seen too many movies. — (M)

ABOUT THE WRITER: Daniel Wighton is an Australian writer focusing on sports, lifestyle, travel and beer. He has been based in Berlin since 2012 but insists that it was only supposed to be a two-week holiday.

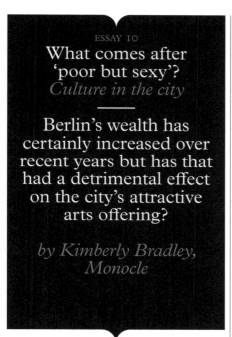

What comes after 'poor but sexy'?
Culture in the city

———

Berlin's wealth has certainly increased over recent years but has that had a detrimental effect on the city's attractive arts offering?

by Kimberly Bradley, Monocle

In 2003, Berlin's then mayor Klaus Wowereit delivered his most famous aphorism to describe the German capital's lack of cash but abundance of soft power and general appeal (particularly in regards to culture and the creative industries): "Poor but sexy." More than a decade later, the echoes of his words remain.

In the intervening years Berlin has become a lot less poor, with more business investment, a booming start-up technology industry and explosive property market. But what about the "sexy" part of Wowereit's statement? Can the city's cultural sector, buzzing for so long, maintain its appeal in the face of the gentrification and professionalisation that are happening not only in Berlin but throughout the western world?

Wowereit's early years as mayor saw him pushing party-hearty tourism but beyond the set budgets allocated to theatres, operas and museums, he was rather laissez-faire about culture, which might have been a good thing. Groundbreaking from the bottom up, the cultural scene was often allowed to manifest in the name of *zwischennutzung* (interim usage). Curators and producers were given spaces to use, such as the central hall of the copper Palast der Republik (the East German parliament building); before it was dismantled the venue hosted performances, an edgy nightclub and a host of exhibitions. Illegal clubs in derelict buildings were tolerated if not promoted. An alternative art fair called ABC (Art Berlin Contemporary) was organised by gallerists without any organisational or financial support. Wowereit's post-2010 tenure saw him hunkering down and realising just what Berlin had in terms of DIY culture and what that meant for global attraction. From this came Berlin Fashion Week, Berlin Art Week and a long list of new grants

"Berlin-sexy is not going away any time soon, it might simply be in the midst of being redefined"

and subsidies for creatives, as well as tax breaks for the burgeoning start-up industry.

We're in a new era now. In 2014 Tim Renner – a former executive at Universal Music and the man who discovered the German industrial-metal band Rammstein – became the city-state's culture secretary. In December 2014, after Wowereit stepped down (largely due to the BER Berlin-Brandenburg Airport debacle) new Berlin mayor Michael Müller took office; his duties included overseeing culture.

The team is working on supporting Berlin's evolving cultural future. With the city no longer poor, Müller approved a culture budget increase of about €49m in 2015, upping the previous allocation by about 10 per cent. While most of Berlin's cultural funding goes to institutions such as the Philharmonic, the opera, theatres and state museums, there's still millions left for individual projects, creative spaces and grants for artists.

Trying to keep things "sexy" is a bit trickier. Case in point: commercial property development has pushed some young musicians and artists out of their studios. That includes sculptor Alicja Kwade, who once worked on Paul-Lincke-Ufer in Kreuzberg but now works in Weissensee in the city's northeast. And some are not so young: in 2014 even star

Berlin's evolving institutions

01 **Volksbühne**
Always edgy theatre.
02 **Humboldt Forum**
This venue opens in 2019 and is slated for multicultural exhibits.
03 **Hamburger Bahnhof**
Still the city's top place for art made after 1960.

turns Thomas Demand, Tacita Dean and Tomás Saraceno were forced out of their spaces near Hamburger Bahnhof Museum. Like Kwade's new space, Saraceno's Treptow digs are impressive but no longer central.

In response the city's new *atelierbeauftragter* (studio officer) is hard at work trying to increase the number of Berlin's subsidised art and music studios from about 870 spaces to more than 2,000. How? By negotiating with building owners and encouraging culture-friendly NGOs – and even the city – to buy buildings for sale and let artists stay.

Some of Renner's decisions – such as bringing in the Tate Modern's curator Chris Dercon to direct the Volksbühne theatre (a bastion of political performance, in which Dercon has little experience) at a high start-up cost – have been hotly debated. But an infusion of international expertise and networks might open doors in new ways.

Looking back one can argue that illegal nightclubs paved the way for Berghain, the world's most famous club, now a platform for young local DJs as well as international stars. Cheap spaces in Mitte in the early 1990s allowed many top galleries to establish themselves but these now support young curators and artists. Berlin-sexy is not going away anytime soon, it might simply be in the midst of being redefined: sexy can be both haute couture and street.

One thing's for certain: in the next few years Berlin's cultural world will be the furthest thing from boring. All that's left is to come up with a new slogan and perhaps consider using the empty Berlin airport as the world's largest and most unusual cultural centre. It does look a little like the New National Gallery if you squint. — (M)

ESSAY II
All aboard
Berlin's transport network
——
Welcoming, efficient and more than reasonably priced, the city's public transport is a pleasure to experience. Just watch out for concealed ticket inspectors.

by Musa Okwonga, journalist

Berlin doesn't have a transport system so much as a series of wormholes, which spirit you across unfathomable distances in the blink of an eye. Its trains are so swift that you may be fooled into thinking that this place is small. And in a moment of hubris, you'll get out and walk. This will be picturesque but, if you're in a hurry, it will also be a mistake. Though Berlin's leafy streets and low buildings sometimes give it the feel of an overgrown village, it's still more than half the size of London.

Thankfully you'll find it easy to make your way around. My own personal favourite is the U-Bahn Line 1, a train as yellow as the iconic taxis in New York. It travels through the city on a railway line raised two storeys high, the effect being one of a pleasantly meandering fairground ride, traversing parks, rivers and concrete plains on its journey between east and west.

Narrowly behind that there's the S-Bahn, the overground train that circles

ABOUT THE WRITER: Kimberly Bradley, MONOCLE's Vienna correspondent, was our Berlin correspondent from 2012 to 2015. She still lurks in the German capital when not in Austria.

Berlin until the early hours on weekdays and all night at the weekend. This line takes you from the city's greyest enclaves to its greenest woodland in just 40 minutes, through the heartlands of oblivious revellers and their grumbling suburban neighbours. On the S-Bahn you'll meet a whole gallery of characters: last year a friend encountered a man who had tethered his pet to one of the train's poles, which would not have been so remarkable were the pet not a pony.

Berlin's trains are, on the face of it, uniquely welcoming places. There are no ticket barriers so during winter you'll often find homeless people huddled in the corner of a carriage for warmth. That's not to say that these vehicles are not soundly policed, though. Ticket inspectors here are some of the most devious and dramatic of their type anywhere in the world. Just after the doors slide shut and the trains move off, that fashionably dressed woman to your left – who looks as though she's on her way to or from a techno rave – will pull out a ticket machine and ask to see your pass. This plainclothes strategy is both startling and hugely effective, resulting in instant fines of €60. Given the cheapness of public transport – you can buy a monthly pass for as little as €60 – fare dodging seems like an unnecessary and uncharitable risk. In such a context you can also see why cab drivers are often unhappy: locals hardly use them with so many cheaper alternatives – including the typically tattered bicycle – so readily available.

It's an apparent paradox that a city so frequently perceived as sleepy should be so quick in getting you from A to B. Berlin

> *"Large and lumbering, their voyages are long and ponderous, they are the sperm whales of the transport kingdom"*

has two airports and would have a third if the Berlin-Brandenburg project had not been infamously delayed. It also has buses that make short work of its backstreets, and which are a lifeline if you find yourself stranded far from your *kiez* (neighbourhood) after a few too many drinks on a weeknight.

Perhaps the true rewards, though, are when you learn the tram routes. To many they are the town's backbone, weaving along avenues or up the city's few hills, trundling towards the outskirts. Large and lumbering, their voyages long and ponderous, they are the sperm whales of the transport kingdom.

Every now and then, however, the public transport here chooses to succumb to the dreaded engineering works, mostly without warning. At such times the city seems to triple in size, as simple journeys now take three or four changes. This happens periodically, as if the city itself is warning you not to become too complacent, not to assume that its charms will always be so easily available to you. Soon enough, though, the trams and trains rumble back into service and this city, this vast village, huddles itself together again, as if seeking warmth. — (M)

Transport tips

01 Close enough
Most places are a half-hour journey away.
02 Street talent
Don't be alarmed by buskers; they're usually pretty good.
03 Flying free
Need to get to Berlin Schönefeld Airport quickly? Avoid the S9 train.

ABOUT THE WRITER: Berlin-based Musa Okwonga is a poet, journalist, musician and public-relations consultant. He is the author of two books about football and one collection of poetry, and writes regularly for ESPN, *The Economist* and *The New Statesman*.

ESSAY 12
Phoenix rising
Architecture in Berlin

Postwar Berlin offered a clean slate to the world's leading architects. Projects such as the Hansaviertel rebuild demonstrate how having nothing to lose has had surprising – and innovative – results.

by Marie-Sophie Schwarzer, Monocle

Berlin was built on a pile of rubble. Scratch the surface and you'll find heaps of debris buried underneath its verdant parks and neatly paved streets. Only about a third of the city survived the Second World War and the rest was pulverised. In the capital alone, 75 million cubic metres of material fell to the ground.

After the last bombs rained down, civilians began clearing up. The Soviet sector made it impossible to discard the detritus from West Berlin in the countryside so it was hidden in plain sight instead, incorporated into the landscape.

One third of the wreckage is buried beneath the 115-metre-high Teufelsberg in Grunewald, aptly called "Devil's Mountain". A portion of its base originated from the Hansaviertel *(see page 107)*, situated between Tiergarten and the Spree River in Mitte.

Once a vibrant Jewish quarter, dotted with elaborate 19th-century Gründerzeit mansions and home to the likes of revolutionary socialist Rosa Luxemburg and poet Else Lasker-Schüler, all that was left of the area by 1945 was dust: nine in 10 buildings had been destroyed. But not for long.

The arrival of the Cold War led to a rebuilding spree, fuelled by the battle of political ideologies. East Berlin began reconstructing first, unveiling grand workers' palaces along what is now the Karl-Marx-Allee, designed to celebrate the burgeoning GDR and its socialist values. The West responded by rebuilding the 18-hectare Hansaviertel.

In true democratic fashion the Federal Republic hosted the 1957 International Building Exhibition (IBA '57), which brought together 53 architects to create the city of tomorrow on yesterday's rubble.

Modern housing estates not to miss
---
01 **Siedling Schillerpark**
Mitte (1924 to 1930).
02 **Grosssiedlung Siemensstadt**
Charlottenburg-Wilmersdorf (1929 to 1934).
03 **Wohnstadt Carl Legien**
Pankow (1928 to 1930).

Among the team were Oscar Niemeyer from Brazil, Arne Jacobsen from Denmark, Bauhaus founder Walter Gropius and Swiss-French modernist Le Corbusier. They grasped at the opportunity to break with the past and reconstructed the Hansaviertel as a revolutionary housing estate that would act as a beacon of freedom, towering above the communist Eastern Bloc.

The high-rises, bungalows and green spaces that took shape were in line with a new model of urban living: a concept inspired by Le Corbusier's idea that a house is "a machine for living in" and the "light, air and sun" principle of Germany's New Objectivity movement, as embodied by the post-First World War, Unesco-listed housing estates such as the Hufeisensiedlung *(see page 107)* and Grosssiedlung Siemensstadt.

The project sums up what lends Berlin its edge: the city doesn't shy away from trying something new because historically it had nothing to lose. And even though this thinking led to the creation of some soulless pieces of architecture, it also gave rise to innovation.

Thirty-six buildings make up the Hansaviertel, including a library, shopping centre, nursery and two churches. In line with the West's political standpoint, the units were laid out organically to embody the new-found liberty of the people, in stark contrast to the soldierly rows of housing found in the industrial age and beyond the border to the East. Instead of dark tenements, the Hansaviertel is dotted with bright homes that were once considered social housing and are now prime real estate under heritage protection.

"The units were laid out organically to embody the newfound liberty of the people"

Despite being more than half a century old – and to be fair, in need of some TLC – the apartment blocks, some of which evoke Cubism with their angular silhouettes, have lost none of their relevance. Furnished with floor heating, customisable living spaces and balconies, each unit is functional and contemporary. Paired with the luscious park landscape that German-born Herta Hammerbacher designed and its connection to the U-Bahn, it's truly an oasis of modern living a stone's throw from the city centre.

Just like the Karl-Marx-Allee, the Hansaviertel embodied a testament to the political future of the nation. And while both architectural milestones have stood the test of time, only the latter is as modern today as it was in 1957. — (M)

ABOUT THE WRITER: Marie-Sophie Schwarzer is an associate editor at MONOCLE. As a native German living in London, being able to return to her home country for this travel guide was a treat. Her dream is to one day own an apartment in Berlin's Hansaviertel.

Culture
— Show
stoppers

Berlin's cultural landscape is always in flux but some large shifts have occurred recently. The city's many established operas and theatres (so numerous, in part, because Berlin was split in two for decades) and 170-odd museums are going strong but new on the horizon is the Humboldtforum, a controversial cultural centre under construction on the site of the East German parliament building. There have also been a number of international appointments that have shaken up the industry, such as former Tate Modern director Chris Dercon taking over the reins at the Volksbühne theatre.

Beyond the institutions, Berlin wouldn't be Berlin without its edginess and interdisciplinarity. Luckily the city's famous autonomous creative scene keeps going, although it's not nearly as cheap to live here for artists and performers as it once was. The next few pages cover vibrant cultural scenes, mixing high and low, institutional and DIY, and top-down with bottom-up.

Public art spaces
Best on show

Open dialogue — The Haus's exhibitions challenge and provoke

①
Haus am Waldsee,
Steglitz-Zehlendorf
Postwar hotspot

In Berlin's postwar years Haus am Waldsee, founded in 1946, was one of the hottest spots to see contemporary-art shows. These days the Steglitz-Zehlendorf location might be a bit out of the way but the programming is spot on: the Haus mounts impressive exhibitions along with concerts, performance and sound art. Its always-intriguing 10,000 sq m sculpture park frequently rotates artworks and a plucky offering underscores its legacy and continuing relevance.
30 Argentinische Allee, 14163
+49 (0)30 801 8935
hausamwaldsee.de

② Akademie der Künste,
Mitte and Tiergarten
Old-school academy

Founded in 1696, the Akademie is one of the oldest cultural institutions in Europe. Today it spans two locations (rebuilt on either side of the Berlin Wall, they joined forces after its fall) and is a place for discourse on new and emerging trends in everything from architecture, visual art and music to literature and film.

Its 400 international members keep things lively with concerts, debates and prizes for art and literature. The Akademie's glass-fronted Pariser Platz branch occupies a prime location near the Brandenburg Gate, while the Hanseatenweg venue is a sharply designed modernist building created from 1958 (and completed in 1960).

The academy also boasts an important multidisciplinary archive of 20th-century art. With more than 1,200 bequests by artists, it has an extensive art collection and library that is open to the public on request.
4 Pariser Platz, 10117
+49 (0)30 200 571 000;
10 Hanseatenweg, 10557
+49 (0)30 200 572 000
adk.de

③ Savvy Contemporary, Wedding
Where east meets west

At Savvy Contemporary artists and curators address and challenge issues surrounding the development of western and eastern art. Founder Bonaventure Soh Bejeng Ndikung, a biochemist from Cameroon, has nurtured Savvy since 2009. The "lab of conceptual, intellectual, artistic and cultural development" has recently moved to Silent Green, a mixed-use art space in a former crematorium in the up-and-coming neighbourhood of Wedding. There's a residency programme, lively discussions, an archive, a library and much more.
31 Plantagenstrasse, 13347
savvy-contemporary.com

④ Kindl Centre for Contemporary
Art, Neukölln
Fermenting art forms

Part of Kindl Centre for Contemporary Art opened in a sprawling former brewery in 2014 to much fanfare. Swiss-German owners Burkhard Varnholt and Salome Grisard gradually refurbished the remaining spaces in this listed red-brick complex and the fully revamped centre finally opened in 2016 with an exhibition by Belgian video artist David Claerbout in the brewery's Boiler House. A new café called König Otto (King Otto) opened at the same time.
2 Am Sudhaus, 12053
+49 (0)30 832 159 120
kindl-berlin.com

Culture clash
The Berlin Biennale was born at KW in 1996

⑤
Kunst-Werke Institute for
Contemporary Art, Mitte
Good spread

After the fall of the Berlin Wall this former margarine factory sat derelict on Auguststrasse, one of the main drags in residential Berlin-Mitte. Not long after, Klaus Biesenbach (now a curator at PS1 and MoMA in New York) and a group of arty friends founded Kunst-Werke (KW for short) and mounted temporary exhibitions (Marina Abramovic is a long-term partner and Hedi Slimane once held an exhibition here). They also planted the seeds for the Berlin Biennale, the first edition of which was anchored here in 1996.

Since then KW has evolved into one of the city's most important venues for experimental art, with edgy exhibitions, film screenings and lively talks. Its welcoming courtyard gets packed during new openings.
69 Auguststrasse, 10117
+49 (0)30 243 4590
kw-berlin.de

I hear Yoko Ono's juggling chainsaws in the nude over in Mitte

⑥
East Side Gallery, Friedrichshain
History in pictures

The longest remaining part of
the Berlin Wall stretches more
than 1.3km along the Spree. In
1990, shortly after reunification,
some 118 artists from 21 countries
brought life to its eastern-facing
section. The unusual structure
is now considered the world's
largest open-air gallery and serves
as a memorial of freedom.

Ironically (but understandably),
plans are in place to erect a wall
to protect the Wall as it's under
constant threat from property
developers, neglect and souvenir
hunters. Iconic art along its length
includes Russian artist Dmitri
Vrubel's fraternal communist
kiss painting ("My God, Help
Me to Survive This Deadly Love")
and the East German-made
Trabant car "busting" through
the east-west divide.
3-100 Mühlenstrasse, 10243
+49 (0)30 251 7159
eastsidegallery-berlin.de

⑦
Sammlung Boros, Mitte
Tower power

In 2003 Christian Boros purchased
a gargantuan war bunker built
during the Third Reich; in the past
it had served as a tropical-fruit
storage facility and a techno club.

Now its 120 rooms have
been carved into a multistorey
exhibition venue with 80 spaces
in which selected works from
Boros's 500-strong collection are
displayed. Visits are only possible
on weekends via prebooked guided
tours but you'll be able to see work
by Damien Hirst, Ai Weiwei, Olafur
Eliasson and Dirk Bell among
others in a unique setting.
20 Reinhardtstrasse, 10117
+49 (0)30 2759 4065
sammlung-boros.de

 ⑧
Julia Stoschek Collection, Mitte
Future projections

Germany's most visible young
female collector – whose
foundation and exhibition space
in Düsseldorf focuses on cutting-
edge video art and photography –
has opened a temporary gallery in
Berlin in 2016.

At a sprawling communist-
era venue on Leipziger Strasse,
Stoschek's gallery rotates works
from her vast collection by
European and US artists. Expect
to see video and single and multiple
projections of analogue and digital
film material from the 1960s to the
present day.
60 Leipziger Strasse, 10117
+49 (0)30 921 062 460
jsc.berlin.de

In private hands

Private collectors are
increasingly exhibiting their
stock in Berlin. An early
pioneer was Sammlung
Hoffmann, a two-storey gallery
in an industrial space in Mitte
that has been showing the
revolving collection of Erika
Hoffmann and her late
husband Rolf since 1997.
It has been joined by Me
Collectors Room, where
international private art
collectors can present
their treasures.

Then there is the excellent
Sammlung Haubrok, which
opened in 2013 in a former
car-service station in the city's
far east, and the Feuerle
Collection with contemporary
art and Imperial Chinese
furniture based in a wartime
telecommunications bunker
in Kreuzberg. Most private
collectors open their doors
by appointment only on
specific days.
sammlung-hoffmann.de;
me-berlin.com;
haubrok.org;
thefeuerlecollection.org

Commercial galleries
Art in the city

① Koch Oberhuber Wolff, Mitte
Making a point

One of the few galleries to focus entirely on social and political art, "Kow" (short for Koch Oberhuber Wolff, the last names of the original founders) launched in 2009. Berlin architect Arno Brandlhuber was engaged to resurrect an abandoned concrete structure, which he clad in multicoloured polycarbonate; the entire building now emits a soft lantern-like glow at night.

The gallery's vast industrial space makes for an excellent backdrop for artwork from such notable artists as Franz Erhard Walther and Russian art collective Chto Delat.
9 Brunnenstrasse, 10119
+49 (0)30 3116 6770
kow-berlin.info

② Blain | Southern, Tiergarten
Go British in Berlin

British art dealers Harry Blain and Graham Southern run this jaw-dropping gallery as a branch of their influential London venue. It occupies an extensive light-filled space that was once the printing hall of *Der Tagesspiegel* newspaper.

A bridge over the main gallery allows for aerial views of the work on show. The gallery represents 31 contemporary artists such as Tim Noble and Sue Webster, Lucian Freud, Bill Viola and Wim Wenders, whose works can often be seen in this lovely space.
77–87 Potsdamer Strasse, 10785
+49 (0)30 644 931 510
blainsouthern.com

③ Sprüth Magers, Mitte
Double deal

Monika Sprüth and Philomene Magers first joined forces as gallerists in 1998 and have been on a high-powered blue-chip trajectory ever since, with locations (at various times) in London, Berlin and now Los Angeles.

Their airy, multistorey Berlin outpost opened in 2008 in a former dancehall and quickly established itself as a groundbreaking art powerhouse. The gallery prides itself on nurturing artists' careers and has long supported women in the art world such as Cindy Sherman and Jenny Holzer; other big names such as Cyprien Gaillard, John Baldessari, Thomas Demand and Joseph Kosuth are shown here too.

Check out Image Movement, the film and record shop next door, which screens and stocks art films.
18 Oranienburger Strasse, 10178
+49 (0)30 2888 4030
spruethmagers.com

④
Neugerriemschneider, Mitte
Heavy hitters

Tim Neuger and Burkhard Riemschneider have been central to the art scene since they opened their first Charlottenburg-based gallery in 1994. They moved in 1998 and are now settled in Mitte directly behind the KW Institute for Contemporary Art (*see page 91*).

Neugerriemschneider is best known for showing big guns such as Olafur Eliasson, Wolfgang Tillmans, Ai Weiwei, Isa Genzken and Franz Ackermann. The two gallerists were also seminal in getting Berlin art events such as the ABC art fair and Gallery Weekend under way.
155 Linienstrasse, 10115
+49 (0)30 2887 7277

⑤
Esther Schipper, Tiergarten
Expansion course

Esther Schipper has been on a steady rise since her arrival in Berlin in the late 1990s from Köln. On the artist roster are cerebral stars such as Philippe Parreno, Pierre Huyghe and Ceal Floyer.

A recent merger with Johnen Galerie (which added artists such as the enigmatic Tino Sehgal and Martin Creed) and a new vast space on Potsdamer Strasse

(open early 2017) nail down Schipper's upward trajectory and art-world appeal.
81E Potsdamer Strasse, 10785
+49 (0)30 374 433 133
estherschipper.com

Import Projects, Schöneberg
Technological revolution

A non-commercial curatorial initiative, Import Projects interrogates contemporary life in relation to emerging technology, identity and community.

Curators and founders Anja Henckel and Nadim Samman (*both pictured*) work with more than 140 interdisciplinary artists and collaborators to deliver a rich programme of exhibitions, screenings and talks. Both also have a line in side projects, such as helping to organise the first-ever Antarctic Biennale onboard a Russian scientific-research ship.
10 Keithstrasse, 10787
+49 (0)30 2392 5563
import-projects.org

Museums
Windows on the world

①
Pergamonmuseum, Mitte
Past perfect

The world-famous Pergamon was rebuilt as a three-wing complex in 1930 to house the extensive and breathtaking collections of Greek, Roman and Islamic archaeological treasures. While the monumental Pergamon Altar is currently under renovation until 2019, other attractions such as the blue Babylonian Ishtar Gate, the Roman Market Gate of Miletus, the Mshatta façade and the Aleppo Room, a richly ornamented part of a 17th-century house of a Christian merchant from Syria, are as splendid as ever.
1-3 Bodestrasse, 10178
+49 (0)30 266 424 242
smb.museum

②

Hamburger Bahnhof, Tiergarten
Full steam ahead

Housed in a 19th-century former railway station and part of the Prussian State Museum ensemble since 1996, this is the place to see a comprehensive collection of contemporary art. The soaring main hall has hosted blockbuster shows featuring artists such as Argentinean Tomás Saraceno and Carsten Höller.

Don't miss the Rieckhallen, a wing repurposed from the old railway's dispatch warehouses. This ambling series of exhibition halls features works from the Friedrich Christian Flick Collection, presented to the museum in 2004 as a long-term loan. On view are pieces by every big-name artist imaginable (Joseph Beuys, Dieter Roth, Andy Warhol et al). Every other year the space hosts the National Gallery Prize, Berlin's answer to the UK's Turner Prize.
50-51 Invalidenstrasse, 10557
+49 (0)30 266 424 242
smb.museum

Museum Island

The five museums on Spree Island just north of Unter den Linden are the result of King Friedrich Wilhelm's vision of making the arts and sciences accessible to the public and spotlighting the Prussian royal family's holdings.

Architect Karl Friedrich Schinkel's neoclassical touch is obvious in the Old Museum, the island's first, built in 1830. The New Museum came next but after the war it lay in ruins until UK architect David Chipperfield's fascinating renovation – incorporating the "ruins" into the final exhibition space – saw it reopen in 2009 (*see page 103*).

The Old National Gallery and Bode Museum opened in the late 19th and very early 20th centuries to house classical and renaissance paintings, and the Pergamon came last in 1930. Museum Island, today a Unesco World Heritage site, is a lovely way to spend an afternoon diving into history.
smb.museum

③

Martin-Gropius-Bau, Mitte
Shows for all seasons

Martin-Gropius-Bau, a short walk from Potsdamer Platz, was built as a museum of decorative arts in the early 1880s (one of its architects, Martin Gropius, was Walter Gropius's great uncle). The building was damaged during the war but restored and reopened in 1981.

It has since morphed into a multipurpose exhibition space that puts on more than 20 large art photography and themed exhibitions per year. The museum also has an inviting café, a restaurant and a well-stocked book shop that is always worth a visit.
7 Niederkirchnerstrasse, 10963
+49 (0)30 254 860
berlinerfestspiele.de

④
Berlinische Galerie, Kreuzberg
Homegrown provocateurs

Founded in 1975, Berlinische Galerie is one of the city's gems. Its shows range from monographic exhibitions by maverick eroticist Dorothy Iannone, a US painter and installation artist who moved here in the 1970s, to *Wien Berlin*, a showcase of historical paintings by Egon Schiele, Otto Dix and George Grosz. During the Cold War the building was a warehouse; its renovation has seen the addition of a second level where the focus is on artistic movements such as Dada, New Objectivity and Eastern Europe avant garde.
124-128 Alte Jakobstrasse, 10969
+49 (0)30 7890 2600
berlinischegalerie.de

Walk this way
——
Children can get creative in the museum's studio

Music and theatre
Lively venues

①
Radialsystem V, Friedrichshain
The whole world is a stage

This cultural space opened in a former water-pumping station on the Spree in 2006. The project was initiated by Jochen Sandig, a cultural entrepreneur and former rabble-rouser at Tacheles (one of Berlin's original artist squats in Mitte). His wife, choreographer Sasha Waltz, is also closely affiliated with the venue: her dance company uses it as a performance space, as do many other groups, including the Akademie für Alte Musik Berlin. The programme of music and dance is always interesting.
33 Holzmarktstrasse, 10243
+49 (0)30 2887 8850
radialsystem.de

②
Schiller Theatre, Charlottenburg
Hitting the right note

This west Berlin venue has become home to the Berlin State Opera, while the company's main concert hall on Unter den Linden is being renovated (the rebuild began in 2010; the opera is slated to return to its home in 2017).

Daniel Barenboim has been at the helm since 1992. Classical productions of works such as *Tosca* and *Don Giovanni* are always on tap, while more experimental stagings make an appearance too. Workshops and chamber and matinee performances round out a rich programme.
9 Schillerstrasse, 10625
+49 (0)30 2035 4555
staatsoper-berlin.de

(3)
Deutsche Oper Berlin,
Charlottenburg
Melange of modern and old

The long postwar division is one
reason for the overabundance
of performance venues. The
Deutsche Oper Berlin in the western
Charlottenburg district, for example
(locals jokingly call it "Sing Sing"
for its raw, sober architecture), is
the country's second largest opera
house and is considered as important
as the Staatsoper (which is still
under construction in the east).
The programming reflects a mix
of tradition and experimentation
and the venue is also home to the
Berlin State Ballet.
35 Bismarckstrasse, 10627
+49 (0)30 343 8401
deutscheoperberlin.de

Hebbel am Ufer, Kreuzberg
Three in one

HAU 1, HAU 2 and HAU 3 are a group
of three theatres in the Kreuzberg
area that opened in 2003. The
well-funded and perennially
popular venues are home to dance,
experimental theatre and art and
also feature concerts by avant-
garde musicians.
   Performances are edgy and
interdisciplinary, and often
concerned with political themes.
HAU also has a strong cultural
outreach programme.
HAU1: 29 Stresemannstrasse;
HAU2: 32 Hallesches Ufer;
HAU3: 10 Tempelhofer Ufer
+49 (0)30 259 0040
hebbel-am-ufer.de

Finely tuned

Berlin's Philharmonic orchestra
is one of the world's best.
Uniquely the orchestra can
elect its own lead conductor;
in 2019, Russian-born Kirill
Petrenko will take up the post.
Its home, the Philharmonie
(see page 111), also hosts
visiting orchestras, jazz and
mainstream acts.

①
Kino International, Mitte
Communist-era hotspot

Opened in 1963, just two years after the Berlin Wall was constructed, this was the first cinema in the GDR to be equipped with Dolby sound. It was also where the DEFA (East German film studios) held its premieres. The architecture is delightfully mid-century and posters for the films, affixed as banners on the exterior, are still hand-painted.
33 Karl-Marx-Allee, 10178
+49 (0)30 2475 6011
kino-international.com

⑤
Volksbühne, Mitte
Hotbed of controversy

Volksbühne means "theatre of the people" and this east German venue – whose building dates to 1913 – has a long, chequered history that's always involved the common man. Early productions were planned as affordable entertainment; through the 1970s performances under the GDR were automatically populist and in the late 1980s the Volksbühne company was heavily involved in protests against the regime.

Button-pushing director Frank Castorf has led the ensemble since 1992, staging provocative plays with edgy directors. New controversy has ensued with the city's appointment of Chris Dercon (of the Tate Modern) as director, ostensibly to offset too-high subsidies with increased visitors numbers and new programming. The discussion rages on.
227 Linienstrasse, 10625
+49 (0)30 240 655
volksbuehne-berlin.de

My edgy screenplay is called: 'Adventures at KitKat club'

⑥
Kantine am Berghain, Friedrichshain
Smaller packages

Berghain needs no introduction: the club is world renowned as a temple to techno. What not everyone knows is that in this small adjacent space, concerts are held that mash up acoustic-classical and deejayed music. It's often an unforgettable experience.
Am Wriezener Bahnhof, 10243
+49 (0)30 2936 0210
berghain.de

Zoo Palast, Charlottenburg
Back in the palace

From 1957 to 1999, the Zoo Palast was the main screening venue for Berlinale, the city's international film festival. When the event moved to Potsdamer Platz in 2000, the cinema languished a bit. After an extensive renovation the building was reopened in 2013 as part of efforts to rejuvenate this patch of west Berlin.

The Zoo Palast now boasts seven screens and 1,650 leaning leather seats and is considered one of the city's premiere cinemas thanks to its key location, hi-tech equipment and grand foyer.
29A Hardenbergstrasse, 10623
+49 (0)18 0522 2966
zoopalast-berlin.de

Das Buch

Like New York, Berlin is a perennially exciting city; one that seems to take on its own character in the vast amounts of literature that has been written in and about it. Prominent homegrown works include Walter Benjamin's 1933 memoir *Berlin Childhood around 1900*, Alfred Döblin's novel about a murderer, *Berlin Alexanderplatz* (1929) and Christopher Isherwood's semi-autobiographical 1939 novella *Goodbye to Berlin*. And then there are the writings of Christa Wolf, one of the steady, strong and critical voices of the GDR period. A more recent noteworthy voice is recent Nobel prizewinner Herta Müller.

Several Berlin venues celebrate and nurture literature, including the Literarisches Colloquium, a grand villa in the city's far west. There's also Charlottenburg's Literaturhaus, which hosts readings and writing workshops.
lcb.de;
literaturhaus-berlin.de;
literaturfestival.com

②

Babylon Kino, Mitte
Small and artsy

Babylon was built as a silent-film cinema in the 1920s, used as a normal cinema during the GDR era and closed due to crumbling and damage in the early 1990s. It was restored and renewed eight years later and has been a favourite arthouse cinema in fashionable Mitte ever since.

Monthly event "Videoart at Midnight", in which big-name artists screen films normally seen in museums and personally discuss them after the film, is always fun.
30 Rosa-Luxemburg-Strasse, 10178
+49 (0)30 242 5969
babylonberlin.de

Berlin on film

Think of German cinema and certain images are likely to arise: Marlene Dietrich, 1922's *Nosferatu*, Wim Wenders' black-and-white Berlin in *Wings of Desire* and a red-haired woman running madly through the streets in *Run Lola Run*.

To learn more about German cinematic history, head to the Deutsche Kinemathek, an archive founded in 1963 that now (since Potsdamer Platz and its many buildings were completed and opened in 2000) also includes the Museum for Film and Television.

German cinema is explored in permanent exhibitions ranging from Weimar and Third Reich-era film to the present. Multiple collections – a total of 26,000 films – are now cared for by the institution, including the Marlene Dietrich archive and the Werner Herzog collection. There is also a library that covers the history of German television and the museum is one of the best resources for information on the German exiles who went on to found Hollywood's film industry.
deutsche-kinemathek.de

Flick fest

Every February, Berlin plays host to the Berlinale film festival. Founded in West Berlin in 1951, it has since grown to become one of the most lauded film festivals worldwide. Wong Kar-Wai, Meryl Streep and Werner Herzog have all led the jury panels.
berlinale.de

Green screen
The cinema is in Volkspark Friedrichshain

④
Freiluftkino Friedrichshain, Kreuzberg
Sunset cinema

When the weather in Berlin warms up, the city's cineastes swarm its open-air cinemas. Freiluftkino Friedrichshain is one of the biggest and most popular, with space for approximately 1,500 chairs alongside another 300 spots for tables, picnic blankets and kids. Programming runs the gamut from Hollywood blockbusters (dubbed or with German subtitles) to German-language hits.
Volkspark Friedrichshain,
15 Landsberger Allee, 10249
+49 (0)30 2936 1629
freiluftkino-berlin.de

(2)
Newsstands, citywide
Off the rack

Where to read all about it then?
1 *Press and Books* is a chain found in most train stations and offers a huge selection of all periodical genres. For more specialised fare, **2** *Do You Read Me?!* (see page 58) stocks nearly every indie, art and fashion mag out there. Then there's **3** *Motto* (see page 60), which sells mainstream and niche art titles as well as books. Or for a reliable selection of reading material over a coffee head to **4** *Café Bravo* at the KW Institute for Contemporary Art.

WHERE TO FIND THEM
01 Press and Books: *Citywide*
    pressbooks.at
02 Do You Read Me?!:
    28 Auguststrasse, 10117
    doyoureadme.de
03 Motto: *68 Skalitzer*
    Strasse, 10997
    +49 (0)30 4881 6407
04 Café Bravo: *69 Auguststrasse,*
    10117
    kw-berlin.de

Media round-up
In print

(1)
Magazines and newspapers
Reading material

Although Hamburg – and to a lesser extent Munich – are considered Germany's traditional print-media cities, Berlin is giving both a run for their money, especially in the indie-magazine scene. **1** *Zitty* was founded as an alternative biweekly in 1977 with listings and commentary; it went weekly in 2015. **2** *ExBerliner* is a monthly expat magazine that covers city events and issues in English. **3** *Aviv* is a text-driven, bilingual (German and Hebrew) literature and arts title that fosters cultural exchange. The edgy indie **4** *032c* has become a Berlin institution with groundbreaking graphic design and think stories on culture, while **5** *Cicero*, launched in 2004, is modelled on *The New Yorker* and *The Atlantic* and covers political thought in longform. **6** *Sleek* is a

sexy glossy covering fashion, art and other cool things. In terms of news there's **7** *Die Welt*, a national newspaper on the conservative side and **8** *Der Tagesspiegel*, a solid local take on all things Berlin and beyond. **9** *Spike Art Quarterly* is a bilingual (English and German) arts round-up. Finally there's **10** *Spex*, a legendary music magazine that began in Köln in the 1980s and moved to Berlin in 2007. It has launched the careers of more than a few pop-philosopher types.

Monocle 24
———
It would be remiss not to mention Monocle's own radio station, which features programmes ranging from daily news to our own design show *Section D*. Listen online at *monocle.com/radio* or download the podcasts from iTunes or SoundCloud.

Radio

01 RBB Kulturradio: This state-funded multichannel station broadcasts in Berlin and Potsdam. Its Kulturradio station runs the gamut of art criticism and cultural commentary to radio plays. The music offering skews classical but includes genre-crossing jazz too.
kulturradio.de

02 Multicult.fm: Berlin's foremost station for world music and the home of shows *BalkanCult*, *Latin Beat*, *Rocking Pogoda* (in Chinese) and *Ngoma* (in Swahili).
multicult.fm

03 Flux FM: For the latest in German alternative punk and electronic music, find 100.6FM on your dial.
fluxfm.de

Design and architecture
—— City revival

Berlin is an open history book. There are few cities that have undergone as many reincarnations as the German capital and its architecture tells its story. Traces of the Kingdom of Prussia, the German empire, the Weimar Republic, war-torn and divided Berlin and the reunified Federal Republic are hidden in plain sight.

Regeneration has long been part of Berlin's history. In the wake of the war, housing estates such as the Hansaviertel – which brought together some of the world's leading architects – were the products of a new vision for contemporary urban life.

There are pockets of antiquity still to be found, such as on Museum Island with its baroque Berlin Cathedral and neoclassical Altes Museum. And significant edifices are being rebuilt: by 2019 the Berlin Palace will be resurrected as the controversial Humboldt Forum, a modern facsimile of the original.

While the ideological and physical postwar division is impossible to erase, Berlin has carved itself a unifying identity; it is, in every single way, a phoenix that's risen from the ashes, ever capable of reinventing itself.

Then and now
Back to the future

① Reichstag, Tiergarten
Room at the top

The Reichstag opened in 1894 as a symbol of Germany's unification. In 1916 architect Peter Behrens added the golden dedication *Dem Deutschen Volke* (The German People) that still adorns the entrance of the neo-renaissance parliament. The lettering survived the Second World War but most of the building was severely damaged and restoration didn't begin until after the Wall came down in 1989. Sir Norman Foster's glass dome, which sits on top of the Reichstag, unifies the old and new. It also affords a great view of the city.
1 Platz der Republik, 11011
+49 (0)30 2273 2152
bundestag.de

Oh, now that's my kind of perch

②
Neues Museum, Museum Island, Mitte
Treasure trove

The New Museum, built between 1841 and 1859, was heavily bombed during the Second World War and refurbishment only began in 2003.

David Chipperfield Architects in collaboration with Julian Harrap retained traces of war damage as a reminder of the past and harmoniously blended 19th-century elements such as mosaics and columns with modern additions. The museum reopened in 2009 and showcases prehistoric objects, antiquities and Egyptian treasures, including the bust of Nefertiti.
Bodestrasse, 10178
+49 (0)30 266 424 242
smb.museum

Historic buildings
Past perfect

(1)
Gendarmenmarkt, Mitte
See and be seen

This monumental square is the place to see Berlin in all its historic grandeur. The spectacular space began life as a marketplace in the 17th century. The following century saw the addition of the imposing Deutscher Dom and Französischer Dom (climb its tower for superb views of Berlin), helping to establish Gendarmenmarkt as a significant meeting point.

One of the finest buildings on the square is the Konzerthaus Berlin (concert hall), designed as a theatre in 1821 by Karl Friedrich Schinkel, one of Germany's most important architects. The structure, which reopened in 1984 after being restored, is undoubtedly classical yet parts of it foreshadow Schinkel's modern style. Come here for organ recitals and concerts. Today the Gendarmenmarkt plays host to many lively gatherings and events; a firm favourite is the annual Christmas market.
Gendarmenmarkt, 10117

Berlin's great but I wouldn't say no to more owl statues

3

Lustgarten and environs,
Museum Island
Park life

The origin of Museum Island – and
Karl Friedrich Schinkel's Altes
Museum – dates back to the 19th
century. Constructed in 1830, it
hosted Germany's first museum.
Inside is a 23-metre-high rotunda
with 20 Corinthian columns that
recall Rome's Pantheon; outside is
the 17th-century Lustgarten, which
connects the museum with the
Berlin Cathedral. Nearby, Italian
architect Franco Stella is erecting
the Humboldt Forum, a recreation
of Berlin's old palace. It will be
finished by 2019 and complete the
historic trifecta once more.
Am Lustgarten, 10178
smb.museum

Royal affair
—
In 1696 Sophie Charlotte, wife
of Friedrich III, commissioned
Charlottenburg Palace on the
banks of the Spree. Berlin's
biggest royal residence is
surrounded by baroque
gardens and houses tapestries,
porcelain, 18th-century French
paintings and an orangery.
spsg.de

 2

Gründerzeit, citywide
Solid foundations

During the rapidly industrialising
19th century the Founding Epoch
style (Gründerzeit) reigned supreme;
four- to six-storey apartment houses
with stucco façades can be found
across the city. These elaborate
house fronts often concealed rows
of cramped apartments – but there
were exceptions.

One prominent example of
a high-class Gründerzeit estate
is Riehmers Hofgarten at 83
Yorckstrasse in Kreuzberg. It was
built by Wilhelm Ferdinand August
Riehmer in the neo-baroque and
late-classical style and opened in
1899. This heritage-listed building
has also been the backdrop to many
period dramas.

Residential
Rooms with a view

01

02

03

04   05

07

06   08

09

10

11

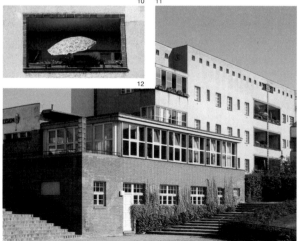
12

13

Housing estates

The overcrowded Gründerzeit tenements brought poor living conditions and disease to the city centre. In response, modernist architects sought to reverse the situation by constructing healthy, light-filled housing estates. The Unesco World Heritage listed Hufeisensiedlung and Weisse Stadt estates were completed in the early 1930s and survived the war. The Hansaviertel was built as part of the International Building Exhibition of 1957 and remains a prime example of modern urban planning to this day.

(Pictures 1 to 6) Hansaviertel (1955-1957): This modern housing estate from 1957 is characterised by innovative apartment blocks. It was designed by some of the world's most renowned architects – such as Oscar Niemeyer, Arne Jacobsen and Walter Gropius – and set the bar for urban housing. *22 Altonaer Strasse, 10557*

(7 to 10) Weisse Stadt (1929-1931): Weisse Stadt (or White City) – named after its chalk-white façades – was designed by architects Bruno Ahrends, Wilhelm Büning, Otto Rudolf Salvisberg and landscape architect Ludwig Lesser. Brückenhaus (Bridge House), which sits above Aroser Allee, is symbolic of a time when living above the street was entirely novel. *153 Aroser Allee, 13407*

(11 to 13) Hufeisensiedlung (1925-1933): This new form of urban housing (named Horseshoe Estate for its shape) was designed by Bruno Taut and Martin Wagner. It was built to be democratic and functional: each of the 2,000 apartments and 679 houses on the estate is as light and airy as the next. *Fritz-Reuter Allee, 12359*

1

Corbusierhaus, Westend
The only way is up

This apartment block by
Le Corbusier (nicknamed
Corbusierhaus) was modelled after
the modernist architect's concept of
"Unité d'Habitation". His "machine
for living in" demonstrated what
postwar housing could look like:
a vertical city with walkways
functioning as "internal streets".

The Berlin example features
splashes of colour that bring life
and individuality to the colossal
high-rise. It is on a hill near the
1936 Olympic stadium and has
priceless views. The Corbusierhaus
remains a symbol of the forward-
looking Germany that emerged
after the war.
16 Flatowallee, 14055

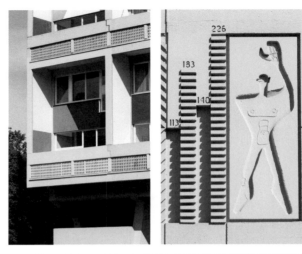

Look around
———
Guided tours
of the building
are available

②
Monohaus, Prenzlauer Berg
Concrete's softer side

Monohaus is an award-winning seven-storey contemporary townhouse made of lightweight concrete. Three years of building – carried out in conjunction with German concrete-manufacturer Heidelberger Beton – resulted in a structure with a light-grey exterior and sweeping studio-like interiors. "It feels very pure and natural," says homeowner and developer Stefan Karl.

The house, designed by Zanderroth Architekten, is one of the first multistorey complexes of its kind but the effect from the street, which is lined with 19th-century residences, is far from imposing.
39 Christinenstrasse, 10119

Cabin crew

Onkel Toms Hütte is a Bauhaus-inspired housing estate designed in 1926 by Bruno Taut, Hugo Häring and Otto Rudolf Salvisberg. It's based on Taut's vision of a utopian society and the name came from Harriet Beecher Stowe's 1852 novel *Uncle Tom's Cabin*.

③
LY43, Prenzlauer Berg
Waste not, want not

The LY43 apartment house is another contemporary masterpiece by Berlin-based firm Zanderroth Architekten. The residence was built to fill an unused plot of land in the popular residential neighbourhood of Prenzlauer Berg; by converting even the smallest patch of wasteland into high-value properties, Zanderroth is combating rising rents and housing shortages in the capital.

The practice employed a palette of glass and wood to construct the 12-apartment building on Lychener Strasse in a gap between houses that measured just 10 metres by 26 metres by 22 metres. Contemporary apartment houses such as this demonstrate that today's city planners and architects are heeding the advice of Le Corbusier and Bruno Taut to build homes that are both functional and comfortable.
43 Lychener Strasse, 10437

①
AEG Turbine Factory, Moabit
Temple of industry

German architect and designer Peter Behrens influenced modernists including Le Corbusier and Walter Gropius. As chief designer of the Berlin-based electricity company Allgemeine Elektricitäts-Gesellschaft (AEG), he was in charge of constructing a number of factories; the most celebrated is the AEG Turbine Factory (Turbinenfabrik) north of Tiergarten. Built in 1910, the iron-and-glass structure improved industrial working conditions and echoed the architectural language of classic temples, signifying a glorification of industrialisation and AEG's position in the world.
12-16 Huttenstrasse, 10553

②
Landhaus am Rupenhorn, Westend
Maintained Objectivity

The cubic country house Am Rupenhorn was built by architects Hans and Wassili Luckhardt in collaboration with Alfons Anker in 1929. It is one of Berlin's most important New Objectivity-style buildings and is off the beaten track, concealed by a thicket of pines in Westend.

This modernist gem was almost lost until architect Robert Wischer and his wife, urban planner Dr Christa Kliemke, bought it in 1997 and restored it to its original state. The pair reintroduced red linoleum floors and furnished the spacious living room with Bauhaus-style furniture. The house is open to visitors upon request (although it's recommended you give at least two days' notice) and is well worth the trip.
25 Am Rupenhorn/161 Heerstrasse,
14055
+49 (0)30 305 9100

❸
Neue Nationalgalerie, Mitte
Art house

This was modernist maestro Ludwig Mies van der Rohe's last major work. It was also the only structure he built in Germany after he fled to the US during the Second World War.

The New National Gallery was completed in 1968 and would have stood at the edge of West Berlin before the fall of the Wall transformed the area into a prime location. The weight of the sweeping steel roof, anchored to a grey granite platform by eight steel columns, stands in stark contrast to the transparent glass façade that allows you to see straight through the building.

The gallery is dedicated to 20th-century art but the interior is closed for refurbishment until 2019. Nonetheless, it's worth the journey there just to view the exterior.
50 Potsdamer Strasse, 10785
smb.museum

Shell Building, Mitte
Waves of pleasure

This 1932 building is one of
the finest examples of Weimar
Republic architecture. The
modernist masterpiece, designed
by architect Emil Fahrenkamp, is
one of Berlin's first steel-framed
high-rises, characterised by sinuous
waveforms and curved windows.
Its dynamic rippled façade is
enhanced by horizontal and vertical
expansions of four wings and five
storeys respectively. The structure
survived the war largely unharmed
and has been meticulously restored;
once home to a Royal Dutch Shell
subsidiary, to which it owes its
name, the building is now occupied
by government offices.
60 Reichpietschufer, 10785

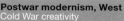

❶

Berliner Philharmonie, Mitte
Harmonious hub

This venue by German architect
Hans Scharoun sits at the edge of
Tiergarten like a retro-futuristic
fantasy. It opened in 1963, when the
city was still divided, and upon the
fall of the Wall it became a central
meeting point for East and West
Berliners. The angular, swooping
structure is largely clad in gold-
coloured metal panels that glow in
the sun. Home to an orchestra and
various special events, the building's
interior is as spectacular as its
exterior; it pioneered democratic
seating that wraps itself around
the pit, giving every visitor equally
good views and acoustics. In
intermissions the lobby fills with
concertgoers enjoying Scharoun's
vision of cultural architecture.
*1 Herbert-von-Karajan-Strasse, 10785
berliner-philharmoniker.de*

②
Haus der Kulturen der Welt,
Tiergarten
Symbol of freedom

Nicknamed the "Pregnant Oyster",
the Haus der Kulturen der Welt
(HKW) was a gift to West Germany
from the US government during the
Cold War and built by US architect
Hugh Stubbins as part of the
International Building Exhibition
1957. It was designed as a postwar
landmark symbolic of West Berlin's
freedom and placed on an artificial
mound so that it would be visible
from East Berlin. Formerly known
as the Congress Hall, the HKW was
rechristened as the House of World
Cultures in 1989.
*10 John-Foster-Dulles-Allee, 10557
+49 (0)30 397 870
hkw.de*

East versus West Berlin

East and West Berlin's design
language reflected the divided
city's opposing political
ideologies. West Berlin, largely
financed by the US, adopted
the democratic, rectilinear
International Style introduced
by US architect Philip Johnson
and Henry-Russell Hitchcock
in 1932 (among other styles);
the state broke with the past by
demolishing and rebuilding en
masse. East Berlin had fewer
funds to spare, which allowed
historic buildings to survive
but also led to the construction
of cheap prefabricated
apartment blocks. Next to
these simple high-rises, much
of East Berlin was socialist
classical in style, which was
more extravagant (such as the
TV Tower) than the progressive
designs of the West.

Postwar modernism, East
Socialist statements

② Urania-Weltzeituhr, Mitte
Time machine

This time-telling pillar at the edge of Alexanderplatz is probably Berlin's most prominent meeting spot. Built by industrial designer Erich John as part of the socialist-led remodelling of the square, the clock tower has been marking off the hours since September 1969. It consists of a cylinder marked by 24 segments, each of which represents one of the Earth's 24 time zones, from Halifax to Cape Verde. Above the aluminium-plated world clock there's a sculptural model of the solar system, and at its base a mosaic in the form of a wind rose.

Next to the Berlin TV Tower (Fernsehturm), which was completed in the same year, the Weltzeituhr is the most significant symbol of Germany's largest urban square, which was named after the Russian czar Alexander I.
1 Alexanderplatz, 10178

① Karl-Marx-Allee, Mitte and Friedrichshain
Berlin's Champs-Élysées

Built in the 1950s, this 90-metre-wide boulevard runs almost 3km from Alexanderplatz to Friedrichshain. Called Stalinallee until 1961, it is lined with "worker palaces", which glorified the GDR's political system before its downfall (its doom was foreshadowed in the prefabricated buildings around Strausberger Platz, built after resources for the neoclassicist mansions had run out). During the Cold War the boulevard would host processions; now it's a reminder of Berlin's history and is prime real estate, especially the Hermann Henselmann-designed domed towers at Frankfurter Tor.

③

Haus des Lehrers und die
Kongresshalle, Mitte
Mosaic marvel

Hermann Henselmann designed
the Haus des Lehrers (House
of Teachers) and its adjoining
congress centre in the early 1960s.
Built in postwar modernism's
International Style, it was a
visionary development that sought
to showcase the GDR's capability
in keeping pace with the West.

The listed building was placed
in a key position, bridging Karl-
Marx-Allee and Alexanderplatz,
and was designed as a piece of
architectural art. In fact, the
façade's mosaic frieze "Our Life",
designed by Walter Womacka, is the
largest of its kind in all of Europe.
The colourful ribbon is made
up of about 800,000 tiles and wraps
itself around the building at a
height of seven metres for a length
of 125 metres, depicting idealised
scenes of daily life in the GDR.

Once home to the archives
of the central education library,
the iconic building is now a
contemporary office space.
9 Alexanderstrasse, 10178
hausdeslehrers.de

Contemporary
Post-reunification projects

①
Bundeskanzleramt, Mitte
Seat of government

Completed in 2001, the German
Federal Chancellery was one of
the most important developments
of its time. It was designed by
local architects Axel Schultes
and Charlotte Frank and unites
both banks of the Spree river,
symbolising the 1989 reunification
and the reinvention of the nation
in its reinstated capital. The
postmodern building, which
includes the Paul-Löbe-Haus
and Marie-Elisabeth-Lüders-
Haus, houses the offices of the
chancellor and chancellery staff
and overlooks the river and
the Reichstag. Its exteriors are
characterised by geometric shapes,
providing a levity vital to a building
approximately 10 times the size of
the White House.
1 Willy-Brandt-Strasse, 10557

I love the
Bundeskanzleramt.
But don't ask me to
spell it

②
Jacob-und-Wilhelm-Grimm-Zentrum, Mitte
Towering achievement

Designed by Swiss architect Max
Dudler in 2009 and named after
fairy tale writers the Brothers
Grimm, this building houses the
library of Humboldt University
plus 6,000 books from the brothers'
private collection; 2.5 million books
in all. The building towers 16 metres
above the city's general height
limit of 22 metres and its gridded
natural stone façade and arrow-slit
windows embody contemporary
Berlin's architectural language.
Inside, reading floors lit by skylights
cascade from one level to the next.
1/3 Geschwister-Scholl-Strasse, 10117
+49 (0)30 209 399 370
ub.hu-berlin.de

③
Jewish Museum, Kreuzberg
Holocaust memorial

This museum, designed by Daniel
Libeskind, was opened in 2001 to
convey the impact of the Holocaust.
Enter via the former Prussian Court
of Justice building and descend into
the Entry Void in the contemporary
extension, from which there are
three routes. The first goes to the
Holocaust Tower; the second to the
Garden of Exile and Emigration;
and the third to the Stair of
Continuity and main hall. The
exterior's zigzag-form and titanium-
zinc shards create a nihilistic,
oppressive atmosphere that reflects
the grim history displayed within.
9-14 Lindenstrasse, 10969
+ 49 (0)30 2599 3300
jmberlin.de

Museums and galleries
On show

❶

Bauhaus Archive, Mitte
Modernist museum

The Bauhaus Archive, originally designed by Bauhaus school founder Walter Gropius, was erected at the edge of Berlin's Tiergarten in the second half of the 1970s. Under Gropius, Hannes Meyer and Ludwig Mies van der Rohe, the Bauhaus school radically influenced art, design and architecture across the world even after the Gestapo brought Berlin's Bauhaus establishment to a close in 1933. Opening the museum in the city that saw the last of the modernist movement was therefore not only a strategic move but also a symbolic one.

In celebration of the 2019 centenary of the founding of Germany's most significant 20th-century art school, the complex is receiving a contemporary expansion by Staab architects, which will enhance the iconic white, wave-like design of the current museum that's a must for any design aficionado.
14 Klingelhöferstrasse, 10785
+49 (0)30 254 0020
bauhaus.de

④
Chapel of Reconciliation, Mitte
Place of reflection

In 1961 the 19th-century neo-gothic Protestant Church of Reconciliation had to make way for the Berlin Wall. Sealed off, it was finally demolished in 1985. Local architects Peter Sassenroth and Rudolf Reitermann designed the chapel that now stands on its foundations. Situated next to the Berlin Wall Memorial, the chapel – made of rammed earth – is encased by a circle of wooden slats that produce a chiaroscuro effect. Rooted in Berlin's history (you can peek down to see the foundations of the old church) it simultaneously epitomises the rebirth of the city.
4 Bernauer Strasse, 10115
kapelle-versoehnung.de

Architecture galleries

01 Architektur Galerie, Friedrichshain: Located on Karl-Marx-Allee, Ulrich Müller's gallery hosts installations by notable architecture firms.
architekturgalerieberlin.de
02 Architekturforum Aedes, Mitte: Germany's first private architecture gallery is found in a former brewery in Prenzlauer Berg.
aedes-arc.de

For more information visit
architektur-ausstellungen.de

②

Tautes Heim, Hufeisensiedlung
Lovingly restored

Designer couple Ben Buschfeld and
Katrin Lesser painstakingly restored
this 1920s house by architect Bruno
Taut. "Stepping inside is akin
to travelling back in time," says
Buschfeld, who spent two years
refurbishing the place, earning it the
Oscar for conservation: the 2013
EU Prize for Cultural Heritage.
Built as part of the Unesco-listed
Hufeisensiedlung, Tautes Heim is
a holiday home that doubles as a
museum (complete with green-tiled
stoves to resemble the place Taut had
envisioned when he built it). To visit
you must book a stay in advance.
43 Gielower Strasse, 12359
+49 (0)30 6010 7193
tautes-heim.de

③

Bocci 79, Charlottenburg
Let there be light

Located in a former 19th-century
courthouse, this showroom for
Canadian design and manufacturing
company Bocci is like something out
of a futuristic Brothers Grimm tale.
The labyrinthine space is packed
with mesmerising lighting pieces
and experimental prototypes
of twisted metal, glass and wire.

Bocci's creative director Omer
Arbel felt that Berlin was the ideal
city for such a project. "Berlin's
old-world energy was the perfect
contrast to the new-world character
of Vancouver; this building is older
than Vancouver itself," he says.
79 Kantstrasse, 10627
+49 (0)30 3276 9432
bocci.ca/79

Memorials
Lest we forget

❶
Kaiser Wilhelm Memorial Church, Charlottenburg
Old and new

Originally built in 1895, the Memorial Church is located in the city's central Breitscheidplatz (former West Berlin's counterpart to Alexanderplatz). The neo-romanesque church designed by architect Franz Schwechten came under attack in the Second World War: the first bomb hit on 23 November 1943 and later attacks left the building in ruins. It wasn't until 1953 that the church was able to hold its first service again and another eight years before it reopened.

The deterioration of the old tower was kept intact as a powerful reminder of the war. Meanwhile, architect Egon Eiermann designed the adjacent church, which is made up of glass blocks assembled in a honeycomb formation. In the octagonal nave of the modern church the glass blocks – designed by artist Gabriel Loire from Chartres, France – frame Karl Hemmeter's golden statue of Christ in an Yves Klein-blue light that's both arresting and serene.
Breitscheidplatz, 10789
+49 (0)30 218 5023
gedaechtniskirche-berlin.de

②
Memorial to the Murdered Jews
of Europe, Mitte
Pillars of strength

Architect Peter Eisenman's memorial was the first project in a reunited Germany to acknowledge the horrors of Adolf Hitler's reign. "First was to establish a permanent memory," said Eisenman in his speech at the inauguration of the memorial in 2005. "Second, and perhaps more importantly, was to begin a debate, allowing future generations to draw their own conclusions. Not to direct them on what to think but to allow them to think."

Just around the corner from the Brandenburg Gate, the memorial – made up of some 2,700 concrete pillars – stretches out like a sea of coffins and acts almost as an oppressive labyrinth. At the heart of the pillars you'll find the underground information centre and an exhibition space that tells the history of the Holocaust.
*1 Cora-Berliner-Strasse, 10117
stiftung-denkmal.de*

Berlin's embassies

Very few embassy buildings survived the Second World War and Germany's decades-long division. Following the nation's reunification and its capital's relocation from Bonn to Berlin, diplomatic missions to Germany flocked to the Embassy District between Potsdamer Platz and Zoologischer Garten.

Apart from the French and US embassies – both of which are at Pariser Platz – many high-profile embassies are located south of Tiergarten. Particularly noteworthy is the copper-clad Nordic embassies complex designed by Alfred Berger and Tiina Parkkinen; the Rem Koolhaas-designed Dutch embassy; and the traditional Japanese and Italian embassies dating from 1942. In total more than 140 diplomatic missions are stationed in Berlin.

Words on the street

Stolpersteine (stumbling stones) are commemorative brass plaques that are installed in front of the former homes of Holocaust victims. Designed by artist Gunter Demnig, they are distributed in more than 600 places across Germany and Europe and list the individual's name and fate.

③
Soviet War Memorial, Alt-Treptow
Strong statement

Most of Berlin's myriad war memorials are known for their subtlety. This is different. After entering through one of two imposing gates of southeast Berlin's Treptower Park, you'll pass a statue of a weeping "Mother Homeland" and 16 limestone sarcophagi (each of which represents one of the former Soviet republics).

The centrepiece is a 12-metre-tall Red Army soldier standing over a broken swastika, cradling a rescued German child and holding a sword. If the overt symbolism is not enough, the site is made from marble taken from Hitler's demolished New Chancellery.
Puschkinallee, 12435

Transport
Impressive infrastructure

①
Oberbaumbrücke, Friedrichshain
Bridging boundaries

This neo-gothic double-decker bridge has connected and divided the city. Built of brick and masonry, with two 32-metre-tall towers with cantilevered parapets, it spans Friedrichshain and Kreuzberg, and its upper deck has carried Berlin's first subway, U-Bahn Line 1, since the bridge's completion in 1896. Considerably damaged in 1945, it was partially repaired and served as a boundary between the Soviet and American sectors until the fall of the Berlin Wall. It was restored between 1989 and 1994, with the addition of a contemporary steel deck designed by Spanish-born structural engineer Santiago Calatrava.
Am Oberbaum, 10243

② S-Bahnhof Hackescher Markt, Mitte
Ornate station

The red-brick Hackescher Markt station is one of the oldest and best-preserved suburban rail stops in Berlin. Designed by Johannes Vollmer and built between 1878 and 1882, it was called Börse after the nearby stock exchange and is an important part of the Stadtbahn connecting Berlin's east and west. Decorative windows, brickwork and ceramic motifs are ornate counterpoints to the functional station designs that followed. The station is heritage listed but continues to be an important transfer point between the tramlines that characterise former East Berlin and the citywide S-Bahn network.
Hackescher Markt, 10178

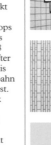
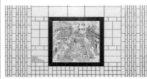

Come back! I have more interesting U-Bahn facts!

③ U-Bahn stations, citywide
Transport of delight

Berlin's U-Bahn dates back to 1880, around the time when the vaulted Heidelberger Platz station was built. Almost every station is unique and reflects its location. Some of the boldest are the work of architect Rainer G Rümmler, who was active from the 1960s to the 1990s; Paracelsus-bad, where intricate black-and-white tiling references the station's historical public bath, is one of his finest. One of today's busiest stations is grey-and-yellow tiled Hermannplatz, designed in the mid-1920s, while one of the most futuristic (and a marvel of modern engineering) is the U-Bahnhof Bundestag on the new U55 line.
bvg.de

D

Visual identity
The look of the city

 ①
City typography
Signs of the time

Across the city, street and metro signs – as well as murals and old shop signs – highlight the different chapters of Berlin's history. West Berlin's street signs feature a modern sans serif style dating from the 1930s, while East Berlin's have a more playful and condensed typeface developed in the 1950s to fit long socialist street names such as Karl-Liebknecht-Strasse.

②
Brandenburg Gate, Mitte
Making an entrance

The Brandenburg Gate at Berlin's Pariser Platz has been a symbol for many things over the years. Commissioned by Friedrich Wilhelm II of Prussia, designed by Carl Gotthard Langhans and built from 1788 to 1791, it is the sole survivor of 18 city portals.

The sandstone gate, crowned by a Quadriga – embodying the goddess of victory in a horse-drawn carriage – was inspired by the Acropolis of Athens. Johann Gottfried Schadow's Quadriga was temporarily held hostage by Napoleon in France but returned to Germany in 1814, where it stood intact until the Second World War. Bombing damaged the gate and spared little of the original Quadriga.

During the years of the Cold War the gate epitomised the Iron Curtain: the Berlin Wall passed right through it, dividing the city on either side. On 12 June 1987, Ronald Reagan stood at the foot of the gate, commanding former Soviet statesman Mikhail Gorbachev to "tear down this wall!" With the fall of the Wall on 9 November 1989 the gate became a symbol for unity once more.
Pariser Platz, 10117

③
Ampelmännchen
Walk this way

East Berlin's pedestrian light symbols – little men in hats – are the brainchild of GDR traffic psychologist Karl Peglau. Designed in 1961, the first of Peglau's traffic lights were erected on Unter den Linden in 1969 and soon they became omnipresent in East Berlin.

Following the reunification of Germany many remainders of the GDR were destroyed but a committee lobbied to save the legendary Ampelmännchen. Since 2005 even traffic lights in the west of Berlin have received a visit from the little man in a hat. Graphic designer Markus Heckhausen transformed the green-and-red cult figure into a brand of its own with shops, accessories and a turnover of €8m a year.
ampelmann.de

Sport and fitness
—— Get the blood pumping

In Berlin, fitness is something other people do – at least that's the way it can sometimes seem. Most of the city's residents appear trim and healthy but your chances of catching any of them within lunging distance of a gym are... well, slim. Indeed, the majority would rather work up a sweat at a club, while a trip to the pool is more likely to mean a sauna and a hot tub than 50 lengths of freestyle.

For many of the city's sportier types, organised fitness comes in the form of football, with five-a-side and indoor matches undeniably popular – but it's difficult for a visitor to Berlin to find a place on a team for a casual kickabout. Also popular is boules but, given that it's possible to play it while nursing a beer, we may be stretching the definition of "fitness" a little far.

But none of this is to say you won't have options: there is an abundance of tracks and paths for the runners and cyclists amongst you – head to the likes of Tempelhof and Gleisdreieck for your fix of fresh air.

Swimming pools
Splash zones

Lap of luxury
The main hall was designed by Reinhold Kiehl

Stadtbad Neukölln, Neukölln
Soak it up

Berlin's most authentic and accessible sauna and bath complex brings a Turkish influence to the traditional German bath experience. Boasting a 25-metre-long pool, the grand main swimming hall was opened in 1914 and adorns many a Berlin postcard. The rooftop terrace provides a sauna, steam bath and a smaller 19-metre lap pool. Nudity isn't compulsory but swimwear is rare – German sauna users consider clothing in the water unhygienic.
3 Ganghoferstrasse, 12043
+49 (0)30 2219 0011
berlinerbaeder.de/baeder/stadtbad-neukoelln

Just dip a toe in. It's not that cold, I promise...

Lakes and rivers

01 **Wannsee:** This is one of Berlin's largest and most accessible lakes. A lido (€5.50 for entry) offers plenty of sand, food, drinks and use of beach chairs for those early enough to snare one. Access is via the S-Bahn train and then a short walk through the forest.

02 **Pfaueninsel:** Pfaueninsel (Peacock Island) is in the River Havel and is a 20-minute cycle then a 10-minute swim from Wannsee. The 1.5km-long island is home to an 18th-century palace and a muster of peacocks. While it may be tempting to get up close to the namesake residents, we recommend admiring them from afar.

03 **Liepnitzsee:** This lake is about 60 minutes north of the city centre by car and is unusual for the region due to its natural white sand and shimmering blue water. The lake is a 45-minute walk or 15-minute cycle from Wandlitzsee station. Once there we recommend circumnavigating the shoreline to find the perfect beach spot before swimming out to the island.

②
Badeschiff, Alt-Treptow
Water on the water

The Badeschiff made a big splash when it opened in 2004 and its popularity hasn't waned. This heated pool floats on the Spree's east harbour and offers epic views of the historic Oberbaum Bridge, with the TV Tower framing out the postcard-perfect scene. As it's exposed to the elements, the season here only lasts from May to late September.

Aside from turning a few laps, bathers also have the option to sign up for yoga on the deck and stand-up paddle-boarding classes held in the harbour. If you prefer less strenuous activity, rest assured that there's ample deck space for lazing – and the manmade beach turns into a bar and outdoor cinema in the evenings.
4 Eichenstrasse, 12435
+49 (0)162 545 1374
arena.berlin/veranstaltungsort/
badeschiff

❸
Liquidrom, Kreuzberg
Sub-marine party

A sauna complex with a poolside bar and underwater electronic music? *Das ist so Berlin.* Liquidrom is one of the city's best bathing venues. Relax between sauna sessions with a glass of wheat beer at the poolside bar; tickets can be purchased for two hours, four hours or per day.
10 Möckernstrasse, 10963
+49 (0)30 258 007 820
liquidrom-berlin.de/en

❹
The Haubentaucher,
Friedrichshain
Regenerated communal hub

Roofless walls frame this lido in a post-industrial strip of RAW-Gelände. The heated pool was opened in 2015 and transformed a landscape of urban decay into an outdoor oasis complete with beer garden, sun deck, sandy beach and indoor concert space. "On Sundays a DJ usually starts playing at noon," says Daniel Lente, one of four partners who manage the venue. "You see a lot of people with kids, the mum drinking an Aperol Spritz and listening to music." There are also fitness classes.
99 Revaler Strasse, 10245
+49 (0)157 8527 9450
haubentaucher.berlin

Flussbad, Mitte
——
An urban-renewal project is underway to open up an 840-metre stretch on the Spree for bathers in Mitte. Reed beds and a filtration channel will cleanse the water between the Fischerinsel and Museum Island.
flussbad-berlin.de

Hotel gyms and spas

01 Hotel de Rome spa, Mitte:
Housed in a former bank
vault, the treatment room
at the Hotel de Rome spa
has a 15cm-thick steel
door to insulate you from
the stresses of the outside
world. The building has
been renovated in recent
years to include a gym,
steam room, Finnish sauna
and rooftop terrace.
roccofortehotels.com

02 Hotel Adlon Kempinski
gym, Mitte:
Berlin's most famous hotel
survived the Second World
War but was burnt down
just days later by drunk Red
Army soldiers. Today the
Adlon is known as the site
of Michael Jackson's baby
dangling and Berlin's most
exclusive gym. Facilities
include TechnoGym
equipment because,
well, you're in Berlin.
*kempinski.com/en/berlin/
hotel-adlon*

03 Hotel Oderberger,
Prenzlauer Berg:
Built in 1902, the baths
became an important
social meeting point in East
Berlin. Reopened in 2016
after a 30-year closure,
the baths have been
converted as part of the
Hotel Oderberger revamp.
hotel-oderberger.berlin

*Uh oh. Where
are the brakes?*

Parks
Take a walk

①
Grunewald
Man-made mountain

The Grunewald forest is just
15 minutes by train from the
centre of Berlin. Teufelsberg
(Devil's Mountain) is an artificial
hill made from rubble collected
in the city after the end of the
Second World War. Atop sits the
abandoned Teufelsberg listening
station, which acted as a US
National Security Agency outpost
during the Cold War. Follow up the
history tour with a dip in Teufelssee
(Devil's Lake), although be aware
that *freikörperkultur* (nude
bathing) is alive and well here.
61 Havelchaussee, 14193

②
Park am Gleisdreieck, Kreuzberg
Rags to riches

One of Berlin's most popular
outdoor spaces came into being
almost by accident. Formed
within the triangle of three railway
lines, Gleisdreieck was formerly
a wasteland at best and a rubbish
dump at worst. But while the rest
of the city was being rebuilt around
it, the area was quietly regenerating
its own ecosystem and in 2006 the
State of Berlin began work to turn
it into lush parkland.
  Gleisdreieck features wide
open spaces in which to relax, plus
fitness classes, cycling and jogging
trails, basketball courts, a small
forest and one of the city's largest
skating parks. There are even
beach volleyball courts, an outdoor
dancefloor and a nature experience,
where kids can interact with the
diverse varieties of flora and fauna
that sprang up here during its
neglected years.
26 Möckernstrasse, 10963

③
Bouleplatz am Landwehrkanal,
Kreuzberg
Roll with it

Football might be Germany's most
popular sport but Berlin's preferred
pastimes tend to be a little less
strenuous and allow for one hand
to be kept free for beer drinking.
Cue a game of boules. Head to the
four courts next to the Landwehr
Canal at the Bouleplatz am
Landwehrkanal in Kreuzberg. If
your own set of boules didn't make
your packing list, simply bring a six
pack and ask "*Darf ich mitspielen?*"
("Can I play with you?").
13 Paul-Lincke-Ufer, 10999

④
Tempelhofer Feld, Tempelhof
Ready for take-off

A former airport, Tempelhofer
Feld is now a multi-use park in the
south of the city. Roughly the same
size as New York's Central Park, it
became the site of the Allied forces'
airlifts, which sustained much of
West Berlin during some of the
more volatile periods of the 20th
century. "Tempelhof", as the locals
call it, survived a 2014 referendum
to subdivide it into apartments
and modern living spaces and
remains the best place in the city
for rollerblading, kite-flying, picnics
and impromptu games of football.
Tempelhofer Feld, 12099
gruen-berlin.de/tempelhofer-feld

Grooming

01 Wheadon, Mitte: On the
   surface Wheadon looks
   like just another smartly
   designed beauty spa
   with a reliable stable of
   cosmetics – and it is. But
   one level below lies a
   small yet smart barber. The
   talented team use natural
   and environmentally
   friendly products from
   brands such as Aqua
   Organic and Luxsit.
   wheadon.de
02 Gentlemen's Circle, Mitte:
   André Goerner's
   barbershop evokes a
   modern version of a 1920s
   department store with
   genteel fixtures and plush
   furnishings. In terms of
   services, customers can
   expect top-drawer
   barbering as well as a
   dapper collection of
   tailored suits, Swiss
   watches and elegant
   shoes. This is where
   you'll find the city's more
   primped and preened
   male contingent.
   gentlemens-circle.com
03 Fine & Dandy, Prenzlauer
   Berg: Contemporary and
   classic cuts as well
   as a customary list of
   spa treatments.
   fineanddandy.de

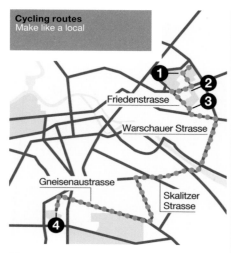

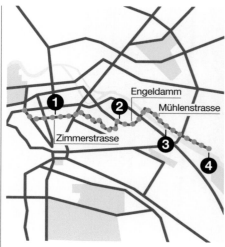

Cycling routes
Make like a local

① Friedenstrasse
② ③
Warschauer Strasse
Gneisenaustrasse
Skalitzer Strasse
④

Engeldamm
① ② Mühlenstrasse
Zimmerstrasse
③
④

① Friedrichshain-Kreuzberg cycle path
Park pedalling

This ride takes you from Volkspark Friedrichshain in the north to Viktoriapark in the south.

STARTING POINT: Volkspark Friedrichshain
DISTANCE: 9km

In other major cities such as Amsterdam and Sydney a district or suburb can be as big as a few blocks but Berlin's neighbourhoods are cities unto themselves.

Start in Volkspark Friedrichshain at the corner of Margarete-Sommer Strasse and Danziger Strasse. Head southwest down Margarete-Sommer Strasse towards the ❶ *Memorial to Polish Soldiers and German Anti-Fascists*. Turn left and head south towards Virchowstrasse and go straight until Landsberger Allee. Take a right and pass the ❷ *Georgen-Parochial and Evangelical Cemeteries* on your left before taking a sharp left onto Friedenstrasse.

Continue straight until ❸ *Computer Games Museum* (*Computerspielmuseum*), upon which you'll take a left onto Karl Marx Allee. Admire the Soviet architecture before heading right towards Warschauer Strasse station. Cross the railway bridge and then the Oberbaumbrücke. Follow the railway tracks along to the right. Turn left at Kottbusser Tor station, following Kottbusser Strasse and later Kottbusser Damm down towards Hermannplatz. Take a right along Hasenheide, named for the adjacent park of the same name, which is one of Berlin's most secluded inner-city green spaces.

After Hasenheide becomes Gneisenaustrasse, take a left down Grossbeerenstrasse, leading you to ❹ *Viktoriapark*. Dismount and walk south towards the waterfall or climb up the hill to take in views of Kreuzberg and the broader city. If you don't fancy the return cycle take the U-Bahn from Platz der Luftbrücke (you will need to purchase a bicycle ticket).

② Berlin Wall cycle tour
Cycle through history

This road follows the Mauerweg (Berlin Wall) trail for a portion of its 160-km length.

STARTING POINT: Potsdamer Platz
DISTANCE: 9km

An abridged version of this mammoth trail is easier on the legs. The route throws up sharp turns at short notice, showing how swiftly and unevenly the city was divided by the Wall.

Start your journey at Potsdamer Platz, where the memorial paving weaves through the traffic. Head along Stresemannstrasse, turning left down Niederkirchnerstrasse and past the Topographie des Terrors. Next head straight past ❶ *Checkpoint Charlie* and onto Zimmerstrasse. A left on Axel-Springer Strasse and a right on Kommandantenstrasse takes you towards the heart of Kreuzberg, now a centre of Berlin's Turkish community. Zig-zag from left to right through Stallschreiberstrasse and Alexandrinenstrasse before arriving at the revived industrial Sebastianstrasse.

A left on Luckauer Strasse and a right on Waldemarstrasse will take you towards the towering red church of ❷ *Michaelkirchplatz*. Veer along the Engeldamm towards the Spree and over the Schillingbrücke.

Turn right onto Stralauer Platz, past the Ostbahnof and along the ❸ *East Side Gallery*. Continue straight alongside the river until you spot the 30-metre-tall ❹ *Molecule Man*, crossing the Elsenbrücke. Turn right when you reach Heidelberger Strasse and ride on to meet the canal. This 10-metre-wide body of water once separated a city, a country and the world.

Running routes
Jog on

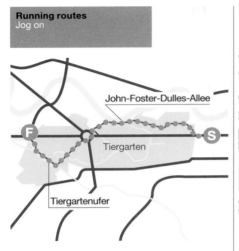

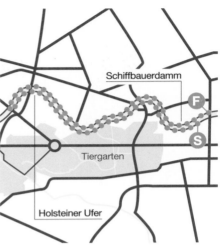

① Tiergarten
Monument trail

DISTANCE: 4km
GRADIENT: Flat
DIFFICULTY: Easy
HIGHLIGHT: Checking some important historical landmarks off your "must-see" list
BEST TIME: Late afternoon
NEAREST STATION: Brandenburger Tor

Tiergarten is the largest designated park inside the Ringbahn and a perfect site for a run. Start out in front of Hotel Adlon Kempinski (where Michael Jackson dangled his son, formerly known as Blanket but now going by Bigi, over the railings in 2002). Head past the US embassy on Pariser Platz before running through the Brandenburg Gate, the symbol of Berlin.

Run north towards the Bundestag and turn westwards at the lawns of the Platz Der Republik. Continue down John-Foster-Dulles-Allee and at the Spree continue straight until Spreeweg; take a sharp left here and head up to the roundabout featuring the Siegessäule (Victory Column). Run clockwise around the roundabout then turn down Fasanerieallee, a tree-covered path closed to motor traffic.

Follow this for about five minutes, past the busy Michael Jackson Tree and on towards Café Am Neuen See. If it takes your fancy, reward yourself here with a drink in one of Berlin's most picturesque beer gardens. Too early? Continue on towards Landwehr Canal and veer right before the bridge along Tiergartenufer. After passing Untere Freiarchenbrücke, turn right towards Strasse des 17 Juni, which was renamed after reunification to commemorate the East German worker uprising against the German Democratic Republic in 1953. Cross the road and finish your run at Tiergarten station.

② Spree river
Water course

DISTANCE: 9km
GRADIENT: Flat
DIFFICULTY: Moderate
HIGHLIGHT: Riverside views
BEST TIME: As the sun is setting
NEAREST STATION: Friedrichstrasse Bahnhof

This route follows a pedestrian-friendly path by the river, steering clear of the busy roadside. Start your run on Reichstagufer, outside Friedrichstrasse Bahnhof station, and head west along the footpath by the Spree. After a few minutes cross the Wilhelmstrasse intersection; a car-free stretch awaits on the other side.

Wend your way along the river past the domed Reichstag (*see page 102*) and around Paul-Löbe-Haus. These two parliamentary buildings and the Marie-Elisabeth-Lüders-Haus across the river are interconnected, as a practical measure for bureaucrats' easy access and a metaphor for a united city.

Continue on the path around Spreebogenpark, past the uber-modern German Chancellery building Bundeskanzleramt and along the outskirts of Tiergarten. While running around Tiergarten you will briefly rejoin traffic along John-Foster-Dulles-Allee. Cross the lights at Paulstrasse and veer right to rejoin the riverside path.

The next landmark is Bellevue Palace on your left, built in 1786 near the Tiergarten hunting ground so Prince Ferdinand of Prussia could live close to the action. Pass under the S-Bahn train line, cross at Bartningallee and again join the riverside path marked by a green triangular sign. Stay on this walkway under Lessingbrücke. Next head up and over the Hansabrücke to the northern side of the Spree, the run's halfway point, then follow the river back east to finish at the Weidendammer Brücke next to Friedrichstrasse Bahnhof.

Walks
—— Find your own Berlin

Public transport might be snappy in Berlin but to truly get to grips with the city you're going to have to hoof it (don't be deterred by the sprawling and haphazard nature of the neighbourhoods). To help hone your focus we've mapped five routes through our favourite pockets and their fascinating street-sign typography, art galleries, independent shops, innovative architecture and restaurants and bars.

NEIGHBOURHOOD 01

Charlottenburg
Glimpse of the old West

Charlottenburg, located to the southwest of Berlin's verdant Tiergarten, was independent of the city until 1920. Known for its large apartment houses and leafy squares, much of its charm stems from the Gründerzeit boom: the triumphant era between Prussia's 1871 victory over France and the early 1900s. The area at the eastern end of the Kurfürstendamm, dubbed the "New West", was famous in the 1920s for its coffee houses and the Theater des Westens, which still stands on Kantstrasse. After partition it became a cultural and commercial hub, home to the likes of the Bikini-Haus from 1957 and the nearby Europa-Center, built by Karl Heinz Pepper in 1965.

Appearances, however, could not disguise that this was a precarious, heavily subsidised bubble of western culture. Pockets of discontent developed, notably around Bahnhof Zoologischer Garten station (Uli Edel portrayed the rampant 1970s drug scene in his 1981 film *Christiane F*). After reunification, areas that were formerly in East Berlin attracted investors and tourists but now the pendulum has swung back. Today high-rise projects (see the new Waldorf Astoria) co-exist with renovated gems such as the Ellington Hotel and Zoo Palast cinema. This walk takes you past these landmarks and along the quiet streets and dappled public gardens integral to Charlottenburg's charms.

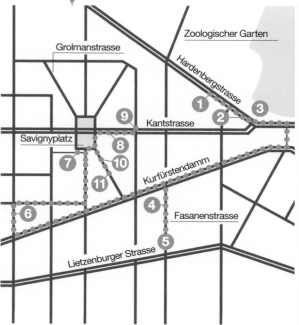

City West tour
Charlottenburg walk

Take either of the main exits from Bahnhof Zoologischer Garten to cross Hardenbergstrasse and you'll find yourself outside Amerika Haus. The low-set 1957 building was formerly a US cultural centre but since 2014 it has housed ❶ *C/O Berlin*, a charitable foundation dedicated to photography. Walk east on Hardenbergstrasse and cross Joachimsthaler Strasse to reach the Zoofenster building. Most of it is

occupied by the Waldorf Astoria Berlin hotel but ground-floor boutiques include ❷ *Hering Berlin.* The dark-wood interior is a superb backdrop for Berlin-based designer Stefanie Hering's crockery, lamps and table linen.

Continue east on Budapester Strasse and stop in at the recently reopened cinema ❸ *Zoo Palast* (*see page 99*), built in 1957 for the Berlin film festival. Next door is the Bikini-Haus, opened in 1957 as a centre for the manufacture and sale of womenswear. An original open "midriff" storey was later glassed over, while the interior was remodelled in 2014. Cross Budapester Strasse back onto Breitscheidplatz to pass the Europa-Center. Turn right to walk along Kurfürstendamm, which dates back to the 16th century and today is west Berlin's main shopping avenue.

Stroll along for a few minutes and then turn left onto Fasanenstrasse for a pit-stop on the winter garden of ❹ *Literaturhaus Berlin.* Once refuelled, head further along to ❺ *Galerie Buchholz* for a chance to see pieces by

leading German artists such as Isa Genzken.

For some quintessential Berliner products head back onto Kurfürstendamm, turn left to walk westwards then take a right to find ❻ *Kilian Kerner* on Schlüterstrasse. It's worth perusing the label's well-tailored, geometrical lines. From here, turn right onto Mommsenstrasse then head left into Knesebeckstrasse to visit ❼ *Bücherbogen* under the old tram arches. The shop is unrivalled for its array of design, architecture, film and art titles collated by mother-and-daughter team Ruthild and Wanda Spangenberg (*see page 58*).

For an afternoon pick-me-up, cross Savignyplatz to turn right on Kantstrasse. You'll soon reach venerable west Berlin institution ❽ *Schwarzes Café.* After your coffee break, cross Kantstrasse to reach design mecca Stilwerk. Tobias Grau (lamps) and Rolf Benz (furniture) also have shops here but we recommend making a beeline for the first floor and ❾ *Berliner Möbelerfinder*, a co-operative of six furniture designers who've pooled their craftsmanship in custom-made pieces.

Heading into the evening, wander back to Savignyplatz and south onto Grolmanstrasse to the stark and elegant Charlottenburg premises of Berlin-born, Paris-trained jeweller ❿ *René Talmon l'Armée*, whose pieces are an enticing blend of understatement and luxury. Finally, for a well-earned dinner, head to ⓫ *Cassambalis Taverna* a few doors down. We recommend the Mediterranean-fusion antipasti followed by octopus or the restaurant's signature meatballs.

Getting there

The starting point is directly opposite Berlin Zoologischer Garten station across Hardenbergstrasse. This major transport hub is serviced by U-Bahn Lines 1, 2 and 9 and S-Bahn Lines 5, 7 and 75, as well as more than 20 bus routes.

Address book

01 **C|O Berlin**
Amerika Haus,
22-24 Hardenbergstrasse
+49 (0)30 284 441 662
co-berlin.org

02 **Hering Berlin**
Waldorf Astoria,
27 Hardenbergstrasse
+49 (0)30 8891 7571
heringberlin.com

03 **Zoo Palast**
29A Hardenbergstrasse
+49 (0)180 522 2966
zoopalast-berlin.de

04 **Literaturhaus Berlin**
23 Fasanenstrasse
+49 (0)30 887 2860
co-berlin.org

05 **Galerie Buchholz**
30 Fasanenstrasse
+49 (0)30 8862 4056
galeriebuchholz.de

06 **Kilian Kerner**
50 Schlüterstrasse
+49 (0)30 9954 3420

07 **Bücherbogen**
593 Stadtbahnbogen
+49 (0)30 3186 9511
buecherbogen-shop.de

08 **Schwarzes Café**
148 Kantstrasse
+49 (0)30 313 8038
schwarzescafe-berlin.de

09 **Berliner Möbelerfinder**
1F, Stilwerk Berlin
17 Kantstrasse
+49 (0)17 3217 7316
moebelerfinder.berlin

10 **René Talmon l'Armée**
46 Grolmanstrasse
+49 (0)30 4989 7768
renetalmonlarmee.com

11 **Cassambalis Taverna**
35 Grolmanstrasse
+49 (0)30 885 4747
cassambalis.de

NEIGHBOURHOOD 02
Friedrichshain
Urban evolution

Friedrichshain was founded as an official neighbourhood in 1920, taking its name from what is now the city's oldest public garden, Volkspark Friedrichshain. Stretching north from the Spree to nudge Mitte and Prenzlauer Berg, unlike its neighbours it was populated by the working class, and home to workhouses and factories. As a consequence it was heavily bombed in the Second World War and when Berlin was divided in peacetime, Friedrichshain ended up in the East. Its urban decay deepened, and even today the abandonment is visible. Sprouting from the rubble, however, are places such as Urban Spree, Haubentaucher pool and Michelberger Hotel.

The culturally diverse community is still evolving, with a rich undercurrent of subcultures and a heady mix of cafés, cocktail bars, independent retail and galleries, making it an excellent candidate for exploration on foot. But be warned: the action takes a little while to kick in and quits quite late. Arriving before midday is therefore ill-advised.

Finally, don't be alarmed if Berliners start draining from pubs and bars near Boxhagener Platz at about 18.00 on weekends. This is purely to evade the international revellers on rowdy hen and stag do's – so do as the locals do and filter into Friedrichshain's welcoming boîtes in the quieter side streets.

Post-industrial promenade
Friedrichshain walk

Begin by taking in the politically geared artworks at the outdoor
❶ East Side Gallery (*see page 92*). This imposing expanse of concrete, which now acts as a canvas, was erected by the GDR to block the view into the West. Large portions of the wall were painted white to assist guards in spotting defectors.

Continue on from the gallery to Oberbaumbrücke (Oberbaum Bridge) and turn left. Just next to Michelberger Hotel (*see page 16*) is Monster Ronson's Ichiban Karaoke – commit this to memory for later in the day – but remain on the left-hand side of the street and walk over the ❷ Warschauer Brücke. Look back west from here for a postcard view of the TV Tower and Mitte.

As you reach the end of the bridge, cross at the lights and when in line with the tram station take a stairway to your right leading down to ❸ Urban Spree. This strip of post-industrial decay has been transformed into a creative hub for exhibitions, concerts and workshops. Pay a visit to the Urban Spree Bookshop for some top titles covering Berlin's street art.

Walk east through the gentrifying industrial lot, past Haubentaucher (*see page 123*) pool and along Revaler Strasse, turn left on Modersohnstrasse then take the first right along Simplonstrasse. After three blocks take a left on Holteistrasse and then head right on Wühlischstrasse. On the opposite side of Boxhagener Strasse is Berlin coffee roaster ❹ Tres Cabezas. Sit a while and enjoy a smooth house blend and some lunch.

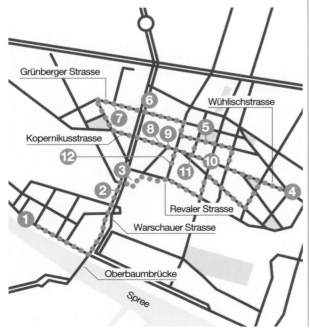

Grünberger Strasse

Wühlischstrasse

Kopernikusstrasse

Revaler Strasse

Warschauer Strasse

Oberbaumbrücke

Spree

Freshly caffeinated, head back west along Wühlischstrasse then right on Seumestrasse and left on Krossener Strasse until you reach ⑤ Maerz, where you can pick up some quality German and Danish threads from brands such as Wunderwerk and Wood Wood. Continue on Krossener Strasse, take the second right on Simon-Dach-Strasse then the first left on Grünberger Strasse. On the corner of Warschauer Strasse is Prague-born bookshop ⑥ Shakespeare & Sons which offers an extensive collection of German fiction and non-fiction translated into English.

Cross Warschauer Strasse, heading further west on Grünberger Strasse and stop in at the regally decorated wine merchant ⑦ Grünberger Weinhandlung. The shop has been a neighbourhood fixture since 1991 and specialises in European wines. Head west, then turn left on Gubener Strasse and left again on Kopernikusstrasse, crossing Warschauer Strasse to arrive at womenswear label

⑧ Corvera Vargas. You may be lucky enough to spot staff adding the finishing touches to items on the shop's sewing machine. A few doors down is comic and pop-culture shop ⑨ Big Brobot. Skirt past the figurines to explore the graphic design and architecture section in the back corner.

By now you may have worked up a thirst; quench it at brewery-cum-bar ⑩ Hops & Barley (*see page 43*). The brewers here shun the latest craft-beer craze, preferring time-honoured German techniques. The result is arguably the city's best pilsner. After sampling a few pints, double back to ⑪ Il Ritrovo – Cucina Casalinga Popolare for pizza worthy of a Neapolitan restaurant, then kick on for a cocktail at ⑫ Primitiv Bar. Reach this reversion to Eastern Block debauchery by heading west on Wühlischstrasse and turning left down Simon-Dach-Strasse. If after some liquid courage you fancy hitting the stage to belt out your favourite tune, retrace your steps to Berlin institution Monster Ronson's Ichiban Karaoke.

SHAKESPEARE & SONS

NEIGHBOURHOOD 03
Kreuzberg
Radical chic

This sprawling neighbourhood south of Mitte is relatively young, having been founded by Jewish inhabitants in 1820. Farming gave way to manufacturing as the industrial revolution made its mark in the 1860s but most infrastructure was lost during the Second World War. When Berlin was divided, Kreuzberg fell into the West.

Bounded by the wall in the north, south and east, the area became a biotope for libertines, political activists and artists. Young people escaping West German conservatism moved here, making Kreuzberg the centre of the student movement and a wellspring of some violent demonstrations. The area's down-at-heel character also gave rise to the largest squat in West Germany, while low rents attracted Turkish "guest workers".

Kreuzberg is still one of the city's most multicultural areas and has maintained its dynamic character as home to institutions such as the Künstlerhaus Bethanien, housed in an impressive building from 1847. Some of Berlin's top tables are also here, including native Kreuzberger Tim Raue's eponymous Michelin-starred restaurant, as well as robust coffee bars such as Five Elephant and Companion Coffee. Although rapidly gentrifying, Kreuzberg's mottled history can still be uncovered in its contrasting architecture, from Wilhelminian streets around Viktoriapark to rigorous Plattenbau at Kottbusser Tor.

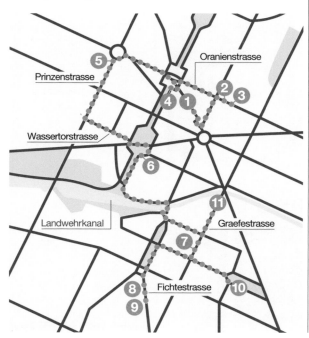

Crosstown traffic
Kreuzberg walk

Start your walk with a drip-brew coffee at **1** *Nano Kaffee*, which offers rotating speciality blends and bags of Berlin-roasted beans to take home. From there, head left along Dresdener Strasse to pass through the imposing NKZ building, where gay bars coexist with Kurdish restaurants and a Turkish bistro. Turn left onto Adalbertstrasse and then right on Oranienstrasse. Walk through a courtyard to Stairway 1 and head up to Level 3. Here the **2** *Museum der Dinge* chronicles the age of mass production, with more than 40,000 objects ranging from pop-culture trinkets to Bauhaus furniture. Next door is **3** *Neue Gesellschaft für bildende Kunst (NGBK)*, an artists' collective since 1969. Enter through the bookshop to catch one of the gallery's politically engaged exhibitions.

Exit the way you came in and turn right past a row of Turkish bakeries. If you can resist the tempting baklava, continue onto Oranienplatz to **4** *Ora*, a beautifully refurbished pharmacy now trading as a café-cum-bar. Everything here is home-baked; we recommend the cinnamon buns. Cross the square to continue along Oranienstrasse until you reach Moritzplatz and **5** *Modulor*. This is a mecca for architects, artists and designers alike, stocking model-making, art and drawing supplies along with furniture and stationery. Walk south on Prinzenstrasse and turn left on Wassertorstrasse. Cut beneath the U-Bahn line and cross the small park until you see the corner block with red

Getting there

The best way to reach
Kreuzberg is to hop on U-Bahn
Line 1 or 8 and get off at
Kottbusser Tor, which is about
300 metres from the starting
point on Dresdener Strasse.
Alternatively the M29 bus
runs from Grunewald
to Neukölln.

typeface reading Gemüse, Obst,
Lebensmittel. Take a seat inside to
enjoy some South Korean cooking
at ⑥ *Core*, where the homemade
kimchi and *yongeun* (lotus roots)
is so good you'll want to order an
extra portion.

Set off again, following the
park south along Erkelenzdamm
until you reach the canal. On
the left side you will pass the
Hundertwasser-inspired apartment
buildings of Hinrich Baller. Cross
over Admiralstrasse and turn left
onto Böckhstrasse, then right onto
Graefestrasse. Here you'll find
⑦ *Kadó*, Berlin's first specialist
liquorice shop, opened in 1997
and now offering more than
500 varieties of the stuff from
across Europe. Turn right onto
Dieffenbachstrasse and left again
onto Grimmstrasse.

Crossing Urbanstrasse will
take you to the tree-lined, cobbled
Fichtestrasse, one of the most
charming streets in Kreuzberg.
Here, away from the artistic hubs
of Mitte and Potsdamer Strasse,
you'll find ⑧ *Grimmuseum*,
which has established itself as an

important platform for emerging
artists. Further south along
Fichtestrasse is ⑨ *Fichtebunker*,
Berlin's only stone-walled
gasometer. Since being developed
in 1883 to power streetlights, the
imposing structure has served
many purposes, including a bunker
during the Second World War,
a refugee and homeless shelter
until 1963 and a food storage
facility for West Berlin until
1990. Double back to walk along
Grimmstrasse then take a right on
Dieffenbachstrasse and walk two

blocks. On your right, across the
road from the park, is cosy corner
restaurant ⑩ *Le Bon*, which is open
for brunch and lunch and offers a
regularly changing menu.

End the walk with a drink at the
incognito basement boozer ⑪ *Bar
Marqués*. To get there head back
on Dieffenbachstrasse and turn
right on Graefestrasse, walking
for two blocks. Enter through the
restaurant, order a cocktail made
with Monkey 47 (a gin produced
in the Black Forest) and recline in
one of the large leather armchairs.

Address book

01 Nano Kaffee
    14 Dresdener Strasse
    +49 (0)30 2520 9838
    nano-kaffee.de
02 Museum der Dinge
    25 Oranienstrasse
    +49 (0)30 9210 6311
    museumderdinge.de
03 Neue Gesellschaft für
    bildende Kunst (NGBK)
    25 Oranienstrasse
    +49 (0)30 616 5130
    ngbk.de
04 Ora
    14 Oranienplatz
05 Modulor
    85 Prinzenstrasse
    +49 (0)30 690 360
    modulor.de
06 Core
    45 Erkelenzdamm
    +49 (0)30 3117 2143
07 Kadó
    20 Graefestrasse
    +49 (0)30 6904 1638
    kado.de
08 Grimmuseum
    2 Fichtestrasse
    grimmuseum.com
09 Fichtebunker
    6 Fichtestrasse
10 Le Bon
    1 Boppstrasse
    +49 (0)30 6342 0794
11 Bar Marqués
    92 Graefestrasse
    +49 (0)30 6162 5906

NEIGHBOURHOOD 04

Potsdamer Strasse
Art of the city

On the face of it Potsdamer Strasse is just a nondescript stretch extending from Potsdamer Platz to Schöneberg but it has been Berlin's main art-world drag since the turn of the decade. The first galleries here snuck into upper-storey spaces or exhibition halls in rear courtyards. Shop fronts remained decidedly mundane – read car mechanics and sex shops – for years before the street's artsy underbelly became visible.

This isn't the first time the neighbourhood has been the centre of an artistic boom. In the 1920s, a collection of galleries displaying art, antiques and Asiatica were to be found in the elegant prewar buildings. But the Nazi period brought an end to much of the art trade and until recently only a couple of venues have been bold enough to set up here.

Today the Potsdamer Strasse art community continues to grow, with many of the city's blue-chip galleries occupying jaw-dropping spaces, such as *Der Tagesspiegel* newspaper's former printing press, located in the courtyards of No 77-87. Smaller galleries dot the street, as well as adjacent Schöneberger Ufer, Lützowstrasse and Kurfürstenstrasse, with more slated to join them. Restaurants, cafés and upscale retail have finally mixed in with the streetscape too. Berlin's galleries have at last found a long-term art district to call home, and it's one with a history.

Gallery promenade
Potsdamer Strasse walk

Start on the corner of Schöneberger Ufer and Potsdamer Strasse for a view of Mies van der Rohe's only completed museum, the New National Gallery (closed for renovations until 2018), before visiting ❶ *Galerie Isabella Bortolozzi*, famous for exhibiting young talent such as Ed Atkins in its unconventional wood-panelled space. Back outside, pass by several galleries alongside the canal and turn right onto Potsdamer Strasse. At ❷ *Circle Culture* see urban art in a white-cube setting; owner Johann Haehling von Lanzenauer shows artists such as Stefan Strumbel, whose cuckoo-clock sculptures are like three-dimensional graffiti. On weekdays grab a bite at ❸ *Joseph Roth Diele*, a homely bolthole named after the famed Austrian author that serves inexpensive Bavarian-inspired lunches such as *käsespätzle* (pasta with cheese) or wiener schnitzel.

You wouldn't know it from the street but through the courtyard portal of ❹ *Potsdamer 77-87* lies an explosion of galleries: to the right Blain|Southern (*see page 93*) and Galerie Judin occupy soaring spaces that once contained the *Tagesspiegel* newspaper's printing presses. In the prewar buildings across the way more galleries, including Thomas Fischer, have set up shop, and the courtyard's deep interior is home to the excellent Romanian gallery Plan B. On your way back out, stop at ❺ *Andreas Murkudis* (*see page 50*), a vast concept shop that also runs furniture outlet AM Möbel.

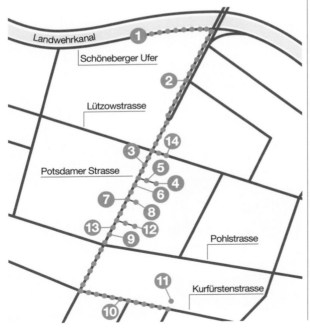

Among other retail outlets settling into the area is ⑥ *Fiona Bennett*, a luxurious hat-making operation that affords a view of its workshop through the shopfront window. Due next door in 2017 is the ⑦ *Esther Schipper* gallery (*see page 94*) in its new home, bringing with it a formidable artist roster that includes Pierre Huyghe, Ceal Floyer and Liam Gillick. A few steps away in yet another courtyard is gallery ⑧ *Arratia Beer*, whose space showcases artists such as Israeli film-maker Omer Fast and Brooklyn-based Patty Chang.

Next, stop into ⑨ *Helga Maria Klosterfelde Edition*, which shows works on paper by artists such as Matt Mullican. Turn the corner onto Kurfürstenstrasse for English gallerist ⑩ *Tanya Leighton*'s two spaces – one in a small shopfront, the other in a white cube – on either side of the street. Favouring Berlin's hottest young artists, this is the place to catch edgy smartypants such as Oliver Laric or Aleksandra Domanovic. To finish off the art tour, continue to ⑪ *Supportico Lopez* in the

courtyard of a complex owned by Scottish artist Douglas Gordon, whose studio is upstairs. You may even catch a glimpse of super curator Kasper König.

After so much art it's time for sustenance. Backtrack to Potsdamer Strasse and dine at ⑫ *Panama*, a restaurant inspired by not only the nation of Panama but also a beloved German children's book. Owner Ludwig Cramer-Klett is well known for restaurant Katz Orange (*see page 27*). For drinks, head across the street, ring the doorbell to enter, and try one of the cocktails at ⑬ *Victoria Bar*. Artsy types gather here in the evening and works by the likes of Martin Kippenberger and Theo Ligthart grace the walls. Those wanting another tipple can head north along Potsdamer Strasse for one block to the legendary dive bar ⑭ *Kumpelnest 3000*. Jam-packed with kitschy decoration and eccentric people, it's not for the faint-hearted but it's never boring.

Getting there

The starting point is slightly awkward to reach when using public transport. Mendelssohn-Bartholdy-Park station is serviced by U-Bahn Line 2 and is a 10-minute walk. For a more central connection, head to Potsdamer Platz (for U-Bahn and S-Bahn), a 15-minute walk away.

Address book

01 Galerie Isabella
    Bortolozzi
    61 Schöneberger Ufer
    +49 (0)30 2639 7620
    bortolozzi.com

02 Circle Culture
    68 Potsdamer Strasse
    +49 (0)302 7581 7846
    circleculture-gallery.com

03 Joseph Roth Diele
    75 Potsdamer Strasse
    +49 (0)30 2636 9884
    joseph-roth-diele.de

04 Potsdamer Strasse 77-87
    Galleries in the former
    Tagesspiegel complex

05 Andreas Murkudis
    81E Potsdamer Strasse
    +49 (0)30 680 798 306
    andreasmurkudis.com

06 Fiona Bennett
    81-83 Potsdamer Strasse
    +49 (0)30 2809 6330
    fionabennett.com

07 Esther Schipper
    87 Potsdamer Strasse
    estherschipper.com

08 Arratia Beer
    87 Potsdamer Strasse
    +49 (0)30 2363 0805
    arratiabeer.com

09 Helga Maria Klosterfelde
    Edition
    97 Potsdamer Strasse
    +49 (0)30 9700 5099
    helgamariaklosterfelde.de

10 Tanya Leighton
    156 & 24-25
    Kurfürstenstrasse
    +49 (0)30 221 607 770
    tanyaleighton.com

11 Supportico Lopez
    14B Kurfürstenstrasse
    +49 (0)30 3198 9387
    supporticolopez.com

12 Panama
    91 Potsdamer Strasse
    +49 (0)30 983 208 435
    oh-panama.com

13 Victoria Bar
    102 Potsdamer Strasse
    +49 (0)30 2575 9977
    victoriabar.de

14 Kumpelnest 3000
    23 Lützowstrasse
    +49 (0)30 261 6918
    kumpelnest3000.com

NEIGHBOURHOOD 05

Prenzlauer Berg
Echoes of the GDR

Prenzlauer Berg lies northeast of Mitte, in what was once the GDR. The neighbourhood is named after the hill that rises beyond Prenzlauer Gate, a remnant of the 14th-century city wall. In the middle ages it was home to windmills and vineyards but by 1800, wineries had been replaced with breweries, helping Berlin become Europe's largest beer producer by the century's end. Countless biergärten popped up around Prenzlauer Berg; Prater on Kastanienallee is one of the last to survive.

After the Second World War, Prenzlauer Berg was in the Soviet sector and breweries and other businesses were taken over by the state. Rather than rescue the neighbourhood's dilapidated 19th-century properties, many buildings here were abandoned and the GDR built new apartment blocks outside for Prenzlauer Berg's residents. The population had shrunk by a third by 1988 but those that stayed were often artists, intellectuals and punks, who turned the area into a counter-cultural stronghold.

It wasn't until after the fall of the Wall in 1989 that Prenzlauer Berg's untouched beauty came into its own. Unlike much of West Germany, it had survived the war largely unscathed and had not been rebuilt. Its historic buildings were renovated and today it's one of Berlin's most beautiful and popular neighbourhoods, perfect for a leisurely weekend stroll.

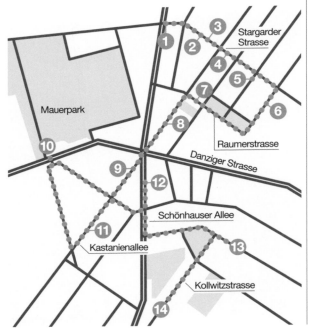

Eastern promise
Prenzlauer Berg walk

Hop off the train at Schönhauser Allee and begin your journey with a coffee at **1** *Spreegold*, a café on the corner of Schönhauser Allee and Stargarder Strasse. Next proceed east along Stargarder Strasse and enjoy the sight of the characteristic Gründerzeit mansions that survived the wars and have been painted in pastel colours, giving this part of Berlin a bright and vibrant look (the most beautiful examples can be found along the tree-lined Kastanienallee but we'll get there later).

On your right you'll come across **2** *Liv*, a shop that exclusively sells enamel pottery; just across the road there's Niko Robert's **3** *Hokey Pokey*. It's rumoured this spot

serves the best ice cream in town; we recommend its eponymous house speciality flavoured with vanilla and caramel crispies. Cone in hand, continue southeast to the **4** *Signore Batistin* deli with its collection of Italian wine, antipasti, homemade bread and pesto. Once you've picked up a few Mediterranean goodies, head to Schliemannstrasse and turn right to find Sabine Geiger's **5** *Present & Paper*. Here you'll find everything from Write Sketch notebooks to Ocelot chocolate, Hay accessories and Caran d'Ache pens.

Return to the main road and take the next right to pick up a new pair of sunglasses from **6** *Lunettes Selection*. Now swing around Helmholtzplatz until you reach Raumerstrasse. On the right hand side you'll see the

historic coffee roaster and bakery ⑦ *Pakolat*. After enjoying one of their 30 seasonal cakes, hang a left as you reach Pappelallee. You'll soon come across ⑧ *No Wodka*, a gallery and concept shop where Aleksandra Kozlowska showcases art and design from her Polish motherland. Next up is the ultimate German experience: ordering a Prater Pils at the city's oldest beer garden, ⑨ *Prater Garten*. Wooden tables and benches, hearty snacks and litres of beer are served in this biergarten, which dates from the 19th century, when Prenzlauer Berg was the heart of the city's beer industry.

After a pilsner or two, saunter over to the famous Mauerpark via Oderberger Strasse. Every Sunday the park is packed with food trucks, buskers and a flea market (*see page 61*). If you're not in the mood for a rummage, join the crowd in the stone amphitheatre for ⑩ *Bearpit Karaoke*. Following a few renditions of "We Are the Champions" and "Satisfaction" – all rewarded with thunderous applause – you might yearn for more polished performances.

We recommend taking in a film at the ⑪ *Lichtblick-kino* on Kastanienallee, which you can reach by walking along Schwedter Strasse and turning left.

Next on the list is the towering redbrick ⑫ *Kulturbrauerei*, reached by turning right on Oderberger Strasse and left on Schönhauser Allee. This old brewery, designed by Franz Heinrich Schwechten in 1878, was turned into an arts complex in the 1970s. It's home to the Museum in der Kulturbrauerei, whose exhibition *Alltag in der DDR* (*Everyday life in the GDR*) is worth a visit to see what life was like here before the fall of the Wall. For more history, stop by independent bookshop ⑬ *Georg Büchner Buchladen* on Wörther Strasse, left off Schönhauser Allee. To end the evening amble over to ⑭ *Scotch & Sofa*, a 1950s-style bar that pours punchy cocktails. To reach it, backtrack slightly to turn left down Kollwitzstrasse and continue straight for five minutes or so. From here it's just a short stroll along Metzer Strasse to the train station at Senefelderplatz.

Getting there

Schönhauser Allee is a good starting point because it is a hub for S-Bahn, U-Bahn, tram and bus connections. You can get here with the S8, S9, S41, S85 trains, the U2 Line, the M1 tram or N2 bus – or, if you want to arrive like a Berliner, just jump on your bike.

Address book

01 Spreegold
82 Stargarder Strasse
spreegold.com

02 Liv
9 Stargarder Strasse
+49 (0)30 3462 7305
emaille24.de

03 Hokey Pokey
73 Stargarder Strasse
+49 (0)176 8010 3080

04 Signore Batistin
16 Stargarder Strasse
+49 (0)30 4473 1492
signore-batistin.de

05 Present & Paper
25A Schliemannstrasse
presentandpaper.com

06 Lunettes Selection
18 Dunckerstrasse
+49 (0)30 4471 8050
lunettes-selection.de

07 Pakolat
40 Raumerstrasse
+49 (0)30 4479 3883
kaffee-pakolat.de

08 No Wodka
10 Pappelallee
+49 (0)30 4862 3086
nowodka.com

09 Prater Garten
7-9 Kastanienallee
+49 (0)30 448 5688
pratergarten.de

10 Bearpit Karaoke
Mauerpark
bearpitkaraoke.com

11 Lichtblick-kino
77 Kastanienallee
+49 (0)30 4405 8179
lichtblick-kino.org

12 Kulturbrauerei
36 Schönhauser Allee
+49 (0)30 4435 2614
kulturbrauerei.de

13 Georg Büchner Buchladen
16 Wörther Strasse
+ 49 (0)30 442 1301
georgbuechnerbuchladen. berlin

14 Scotch & Sofa
18 Kollwitzstrasse
+49 (0)30 6800 4203

Resources
—— Inside knowledge

You've explored layers of history, taken in oodles of culture and perhaps even partied all weekend. Still, gaining a full overview is difficult, even for locals. Here's a guide to what's interesting and important, how to get there, and how to say the right thing wherever you go.

We also provide you with a soundtrack to the city to help you better absorb Berlin's past and present, its legacy and influence. Also listed is a calendar of can't-miss annual events, and a selection of the best places to spend your time in all kinds of weather.

Transport
Get around town

01 **Flights:** As BER airport languishes in limbo, Berlin Tegel is the businessperson's preferred choice, about 8km from the city centre. Berlin Schönefeld is further out in the city's far east and is a hub for inexpensive charters. Both can be reached by train while taxis will leave you €35 poorer. Charter private jets via Victor.
flyvictor.com

02 **Trains:** Berlin's subway lines (U-Bahn) and commuter trains (S-Bahn) are quick ways to get around the city, even if locals complain they're always under construction (only partially true these days; it took more than 25 years to reconnect east and west). Monthly passes are €81, package deals are available for tourists. Single rides are €2.70.
bvg.de

03 **Bicycle:** The German rail (Deutsche Bahn) runs Call a Bike, a bikesharing system in Berlin; parked bikes in stations across the city can be booked by mobile phone.
callabike-interaktiv.de

04 **Bus and tram:** Buses operate day and night; trams are only found on the city's east side but are fast and reliable. The double-decker buses are a west Berlin trademark; lines 100 and 200 are tourist routes in themselves.
bvg.de

05 **On foot:** Berlin is big. Don't think you can walk from major points in the east to those in the west without lots of time. Some neighbourhoods – such as central Mitte or the Kurfürstendamm area – can be walked but do some research before embarking.

06 **Taxi and private car hire:** Taxi fares are €3.90 to start, then €2.00 per kilometre for the first seven kilometres, and €1.50 for each kilometre above that. For a private vehicle, book with Blacklane.
blacklane.com/en/cities-berlin

Vocabulary
Local lingo

01 **Guten tag:** Hello
02 **Tschüss:** Goodbye
03 **Späti:** A neighbourhood shop with food and drink that stays open late
04 **Görli:** Görlitzer Park
05 **Alles jute:** All the best
06 **Schorle:** Adding "schorle" to any drink order means it comes mixed with sparkling water (as in *apfelschorle* or *weinschorle*)
07 **Rechnung or "Zahlen bitte":** Bill or "I'd like to pay"
08 **Krass:** Yuck, OMG
09 **Feiern:** To party
10 **Kiez:** Neighbourhood

Soundtrack to the city
Five top tunes

Berlin has inspired more than its share of music, spanning eras and genres. Here's a playlist.

01 **Marlene Dietrich, 'Ich hab noch einen Koffer in Berlin':** The singer's 1950s nostalgic ode to a city where she always left a suitcase waiting.

02 **Lou Reed, 'Berlin':** This jazzy 1973 tune begins with "In Berlin, by the wall, you were five foot ten inches tall." Lou takes his romantic interlude from there, in his typical spoken-sung prose.

03 **David Bowie, 'Heroes':** An eternally inspiring track, recorded here in the late 1970s when Bowie was getting his life together.

04 **Ideal, 'Berlin':** Neue Deutsche Welle (New German Wave) at its punky finest. Lead singer Annette Humpe's raucous vocals yell in Gernman: "I feel good, I like Berlin."

05 **Moderat, 'Berlin':** This Berlin-based electronic band has a long list of hits but this short riff sounds like an interstellar message from the city to outer space.

Best events
What to see

01 Berlin Film Festival, various locations: One of the world's seminal film festivals. *February, berlinale.de*

02 Märzmusik, various locations: "March music" evolved out of Berlin's former music biennale; it features new and avant-garde music, symposia and talks. *March, berlinerfestspiele.de*

03 Karneval der Kulturen, Kreuzberg: A raucous street party/market/theatre in honour of the cultures of the world. *May or June, karneval-berlin.de*

04 DFB Cup final, Olympic Stadium: Culmination of a knockout competition equivalent to England's FA Cup. *May or June, dfb.de*

05 Berlin Beer Festival, Karl Marx Allee: For a few days a sizeable stretch of Karl Marx Allee turns into the world's longest beer garden. *August, bierfestival-berlin.de*

06 Long Night of Museums, various locations: More than 70 of Berlin's museums and institutions open their doors from 18.00 to 02.00 one late-summer night. Unmissable. *Late August, lange-nacht-der-museen.de*

07 Berlin Art Week, various locations: The ABC contemporary-art fair, museum exhibits, and lots of festivities start the autumn art season. *September, berlinartweek.de*

08 Festival of Lights, citywide: Berlin illuminates its most notable landmarks with colourful lights and beams. *October, festival-of-lights.de*

09 Berlin Christmas Markets, various locations: Christmas markets sell craft wares and serve mulled wine. *Mid-November to Christmas*

10 Silvester, citywide: The New Year's Eve fireworks at the Brandenburg Gate are a treat. *31 December*

Rainy days
Weather-proof activities

Berlin can be rainy and its winters are long and often frosty, thanks to legendary Siberian cold fronts. Fortunately its museums are plentiful, coffee culture ubiquitous and conversation heady.

01 Museum Island: The northern half of an island in the Spree, and just a hop from east Berlin's main drag Unter den Linden, this Unesco World Heritage site boasts five world-class museums. The first, the Altes Museum, was built in 1830. The Bode, Pergamon and Neues Museums additionally anchor the island with collections of classical, Islamic and European art. Other nearby highlights are the CFA gallery (built by David Chipperfield) and a famous weekend antiques market.

02 Kadewe: Continental Europe's largest department store, named after *Kaufhaus des Westens* (Department Store of the West) offers 60,000 sq m of wonders including top brands such as Celine, Hermès and Rolex, high-street fashion like Topshop and one of the world's most famous food departments. The latter is a wonderful place to spend an afternoon with a friend, eating oysters and sampling an array of wines and spirits. A Berlin attraction since 1907. *kadewe.com*

03 Café culture: No weekend in Berlin is complete without brunch, lunch, coffee – or all of the above – in a café. Many Berlin cafés magically transform into restaurants and bars as the day goes on. Dotting the city and often defining neighbourhoods, some are old-school and some decidedly third-wave but none expect guests to leave quickly.

Sunny days
The great outdoors

Summers in Berlin make up for the long, dark winters and as the days grow longer, the city comes out to play. Take advantage of good weather when it comes with any of these activities.

01 Water tours: Berlin has five rivers, six canals and some 80 lakes; boat tours are offered for all of them on at least an hourly basis. Vessels range from semi-public tourist boats to private yachts. Seeing the city from the water is a wonderful way to glimpse another side of the German capital and it's not just for tourists. *visitberlin.de/en/see/city-tours/boat-tours*

02 Beer gardens: Outdoor beer gardens aren't just a southern-German tradition; Berlin holds its own with a number of lovely outdoor venues such as Prater in Prenzlauer Berg, the Schleusenkrug and Café am Neuen See in Tiergarten, and the Pavillon in Volkspark Friedrichshain. In good weather, beer gardens pop up around the city's western lakes too. On tap are Berliner Kindl (admittedly a rather unremarkable brew) but also, increasingly, craft beers from elsewhere in the country and beyond.

03 Get on your bike and ride: Around 900km of bicycle paths crisscross the German capital. Cycling (rent a bike from the many Fahrradstation stores around the city) is one of the best ways to explore Berlin's sights and its many green zones at your own pace. From April to October, Fahrradstation also offers bike tours focusing on different districts and historical eras. Watch for traffic – and be sure to lock up. *fahrradstation.com*

About Monocle
—— Step inside

London HQ
——
Our editorial office is in Marylebone

In 2007, Monocle was launched as a monthly magazine briefing on global affairs, business, culture, design and much more. We believed there was a globally minded audience of readers who were hungry for opportunities and experiences beyond their national borders.

Today Monocle is a complete media brand with print, audio and online elements – not to mention our expanding network of shops and cafés. Besides our London HQ we have seven international bureaux in New York, Toronto, Istanbul, Singapore, Tokyo, Zürich and Hong Kong. We continue to grow and flourish and at our core is the simple belief that there will always be a place for a print brand that is committed to telling fresh stories and sending photographers on assignments. It's also a case of knowing that our success is all down to the readers, advertisers and collaborators who have supported us along the way.

①
International bureaux
Boots on the ground

We have an HQ in London and call upon firsthand reports from our contributors in more than 35 cities around the world. We also have seven international bureaux. For this travel guide, MONOCLE reporters Mikaela Aitken and Marie-Sophie Schwarzer popped over to the German capital to explore all that it has to offer. They also called on the assistance of writers in the city, including our correspondents Kimberly Bradley and Kati Krause, to ensure we have covered the very best in retail, food, hospitality and entertainment. The aim is to make you, the reader, feel like a local when visiting Berlin.

②
Online
Digital delivery

We have a dynamic website: *monocle.com.* As well as being the place to hear our radio station, Monocle 24, the site presents our films, which are beautifully shot and edited by our in-house team and provide a fresh perspective on our stories. Check out the films celebrating the cities that make up our Travel Guide Series before you explore the rest of the site.

③
Retail and cafés
Food for thought

Via our shops in Hong Kong, Toronto, New York, Tokyo, London and Singapore we sell products that cater to our readers' tastes and are produced in collaboration with brands we love. We also have cafés in Tokyo and London. And if you are in the UK capital, visit the Kioskafé in Paddington, which combines good coffee and great reads.

4
Print
Committed to the page

MONOCLE is published 10 times a year. We have stayed loyal to our belief in quality print with two extra seasonal publications: THE FORECAST, packed with key insights into the year ahead, and THE ESCAPIST, our summer travel-minded magazine. To sign up visit *monocle.com/ subscribe*. Since 2013 we have also been publishing books, like this one, in partnership with Gestalten.

5
Radio
Sound approach

Monocle 24 is our round-the-clock radio station that was launched in 2011. It delivers global news and shows covering foreign affairs, urbanism, business, culture, food and drink, design and print media. When you find yourself in Berlin, tune into *The Globalist*, our morning news programme that is the perfect way to start the day in Europe. We also have a playlist to accompany you day and night, regularly assisted by live band sessions that are hosted at our Midori House headquarters in London. You can listen live or download any of our shows from *monocle.com*, iTunes or SoundCloud.

Priority service
Subscribers save 10 per cent online

Join the club

01
Subscribe to Monocle
A subscription is a simple way to make sure you never miss a copy and enjoy many additional benefits.

02
Read every issue published
Our subscribers have exclusive access to the entire Monocle archive, and have priority access to selected product collaborations at *monocle.com*.

03
Never miss an issue
Subscription copies are delivered to your door no matter where you are in the world, and we offer an auto-renewal service to ensure that you never miss an issue.

04
And there's more...
Subscribers benefit from a 10 per cent discount at all Monocle shops, including online, and receive exclusive offers and invitations to events around the world.

Choose your package

Premium one year
12 × issues
+ Porter Sub Club bag

One year
12 × issues
+ Monocle Voyage tote bag

Six months
6 × issues

Chief photographers
Silvia Conde
Thomas Meyer

Still life
David Sykes

Images
Alamy
Archiv Berliner Philharmoniker
Karolina Bak
Sebastian Bolesch
Felix Brüggemann
Liam Gillick
Mila Hacke
Markus Hawlik
Karsten Hintz
Caro Hoene
Soho House
Getty Images
The Kadewe group
Mathilde Karrèr
Alexander Koch
Helga Koppatsch
Robbie Lawrence
Kaspar F Lerch
Lichtschwärmer
Ashley Ludaescher
Manfred Mayer
Maximilian Meisse
Ludger Paffrath
Philippe Parreno
Stephanie Pilick
Michael Reisch
Hannes Rohrer
Ana Santl
Esther Schipper
Schirmer, Berliner Philharmoniker
Zoe Spawton
Nina Strassgütl
Andreas Süss
Federico Testa
Saskia Uppenkamp
Anna Warnow
Harry Weber
Sabine Wenzel
Jens Ziehe

Illustrators
Satoshi Hashimoto
Ceylan Sahin
Tokuma

Writers
Mikaela Aitken
Gal Barnea
Kimberly Bradley
Jessica Bridger
Beatrice Carmi
Melkon Charchoglyan
Kati Krause
Robbie Lawrence
Eve Lucas
Rory MacLean
Charlie Monaghan
Musa Okwonga
Joseph Pearson
Joe Pickard
Antonia Maerzhaeuser
Ole Schulz
Marie-Sophie Schwarzer
Santiago Rodriguez Tarditi
Daniel Wighton

Monocle
EDITOR IN CHIEF AND CHAIRMAN
Tyler Brûlé
EDITOR
Andrew Tuck
CREATIVE DIRECTOR
Richard Spencer Powell

**The Monocle Travel Guide
Series: Berlin**
GUIDE EDITOR
Mikaela Aitken
ASSOCIATE GUIDE EDITOR
Marie-Sophie Schwarzer
PHOTO EDITOR
Faye Sakura Rentoule

**The Monocle Travel Guide
Series**
SERIES EDITOR
Joe Pickard
ASSOCIATE EDITOR, BOOKS
Amy Richardson
ASSISTANT EDITOR
Mikaela Aitken
DESIGNERS
Sam Brogan
Jay Yeo
Loi Xuan Ly
PHOTO EDITORS
Matthew Beaman
Faye Sakura Rentoule
Shin Miura

PRODUCTION
Jacqueline Deacon
Dan Poole
Chloë Ashby
Sean McGeady
Sonia Zhuravlyova

CHAPTER EDITING

Need to know
Kimberly Bradley

Hotels
Mikaela Aitken

 ❷
Food and drink
Kati Krause

 ❸
Retail
Mikaela Aitken

 ❹
Things we'd buy
Mikaela Aitken

❺
Essays
Mikaela Aitken

 ❻
Culture
Kimberly Bradley

 ❼
Design and architecture
Marie-Sophie Schwarzer

 ❽
Sport and fitness
Mikaela Aitken

 ❾
Walks
Mikaela Aitken

Resources
Kimberly Bradley

Research
Gal Barnea
Beatrice Carmi
Jake FitzSimons
Daphne Karnezis
Kurt Lin
Clarissa Pharr
Zayana Zulkiflee

Special thanks
Herbert Hofmann
Thomas M Krüger
Ticket B
Visit Berlin
YSSO

New

The MONOCLE Travel Guide Series 16

Los Angeles

... Ride with us through the city's outposts of good food, design, retail and more. Buckle up! ...

The MONOCLE Travel Guide Series 17

Toronto

... Hello! Skate with us through the city's outposts of good food, design, retail and more. Have a good trip, eh? ...

Buy today at all good bookshops

Or visit the online shops at
monocle.com and
shop.gestalten.com

The collection
We hope you have found the Monocle Travel Guide to Berlin useful, inspiring and entertaining. There's plenty more to get your teeth into: we have a global suite of guides, with many more set to be released in coming months. Cities are fun. Let's explore.

❶ London
The sights, sounds and style

❷ New York
Get a taste of the Big Apple's best

❸ Tokyo
The enigmatic glory of Japan's capital

❹ Hong Kong
Down to business in this vibrant city

❺ Madrid
Captivating capital abuzz with spirit

❻ Bangkok
Stimulate your senses with the exotic

❼ Istanbul
Thrilling fusion of Asia and Europe

❽ Miami
Unpack the Magic City's box of tricks

❾ Rio de Janeiro
Beaches, bars and bossa nova

❿ Paris
Be romanced by the City of Light

⓫ Singapore
Where modernity meets tradition

⓬ Vienna
Waltz through the Austrian capital

⓭ Sydney
Sun, surf and urban delights

⓮ Honolulu
Embrace Hawaii's aloha spirit

⓯ Copenhagen
Cycle through the Danish capital

⓰ Los Angeles
Fly high in the City of Angels

⓱ Toronto
Delve into this diverse Canadian city

⓲ Berlin
Discover the city of two halves

Next stops: Amsterdam, Stockholm and Venice. I've packed light...